The Art *of* Funding *and*
Implementing Ideas

For Laurisa, an accomplished fund-raiser and a wonderful wife who maintains in her work and her life a tight connection among caring, clarity, and creativity.

—Arnold R. Shore

I would like to dedicate this book to the many faculty colleagues and students who, over the years, helped to conceptually frame this work via the many questions they asked about grant writing and proposal development, sketching ideas, formulating research questions, integrating pilot data, and critically thinking about how to best write and position meaningful narrative along with qualitative and quantitative data. Similar conversations around the development of strategies for efficiently and effectively managing a funded project are always exciting to hear and have, as are discussions around international research collaborations. In light of the above, I would also like to dedicate this work to you the reader, hoping you too will benefit from the ongoing conversation around how we move compelling ideas forward and successfully manage a funded project.

—John M. Carfora

The Art of Funding and Implementing Ideas

A Guide to Proposal Development and Project Management

Arnold R. Shore
Boston College

&

John M. Carfora
Loyola Marymount University

Los Angeles | London | New Delhi
Singapore | Washington DC

For information:

SAGE Publications, Inc.
2455 Teller Road
Thousand Oaks, California 91320
E-mail: order@sagepub.com

SAGE Publications India Pvt. Ltd.
B 1/I 1 Mohan Cooperative
   Industrial Area
Mathura Road, New Delhi 110 044
India

SAGE Publications Ltd.
1 Oliver's Yard
55 City Road
London EC1Y 1SP
United Kingdom

SAGE Publications Asia-Pacific Pte. Ltd.
33 Pekin Street #02-01
Far East Square
Singapore 048763

Printed in the United States of America

Library of Congress Cataloging-in-Publication Data

Shore, Arnold, 1944-
The art of funding and implementing ideas : a guide to proposal development and project management / Arnold R. Shore, John M. Carfora.
   p. cm.
Includes bibliographical references and index.
ISBN 978-1-4129-8042-5 (pbk.)
   1. Project management—Finance. 2. Project management—Evaluation.
3. Education—Research—Finance. 4. Proposal writing for grants. I. Carfora, John M.
II. Title.

HD69.P75S535 2011
378.1'736—dc22   2009047309

This book is printed on acid-free paper.

10   11   12   13   14   10   9   8   7   6   5   4   3   2   1

Acquisitions Editor:	Vicki Knight
Editorial Assistant:	Ashley Dodd
Associate Editor:	Lauren Habib
Production Editor:	Catherine M. Chilton
Copy Editor:	Heidi Unkrich
Typesetter:	C&M Digitals (P) Ltd.
Proofreader:	Jennifer Gritt

Marketing Manager:	Stephanie Adams

Brief Contents

Detailed Contents

Preface

Why We Wrote This Book

The literature on proposal writing is vast. Even a cursory search on the Internet turns up scores of books, pamphlets, checklists, and websites authored by individuals or offered by institutions of higher education, government funding agencies, and nonprofit organizations that support research, scholarly, and creative activities. Why, then, another book on developing grant proposals? The answer lies in two directions: one relating to the literature on proposal development and the other to our own experience in the fields of idea development, proposal preparation, and research support.

The literature on proposal development tends to offer and emphasize long lists of dos and don'ts. For example, *do* be as specific as possible in describing your work, and *do* follow sponsor guidelines religiously and explicitly. *Don't* overpromise what you cannot deliver, and *don't* fail to account for every projected expense in a clearly described budget line. There is no denying the value of this type of advice. Yet, its form may be problematic—checklists tend to have an "etcetera" quality and far too often travel in many directions at once—and its implicit message may be unfortunate: The writing of a proposal is challenging, and its rigors are many and not easily surmounted. These nuances, if they may be called that, are not lost on those who read and study the literature on proposal development looking for helpful hints and useful guidance.

We find much of the literature long on advice and short on grounded principles and substantive guidance. That is precisely why we are offering an alternative approach in this book.

The two of us have worked for many years in the interconnected domains of idea development, funded research, grant and contract administration, project management, and developing and delivering institutional support of funded projects. One of us headed foundations and nonprofit organizations that funded research initiatives. The other pursued a long and successful career as a funded academic and a nationally and internationally recognized research administrator. Together, we have counseled with large numbers of faculty, program officers at foundations and corporations, and postdoctoral scholars and graduate students on proposal and project development. Individually, we have written a fair number of successful proposals ourselves. From our university-based work, we have come to think of academics as thematic, topical, and methodological experts on the one hand and as the ultimate lifelong (adult) learners on the other. As the former, the comparative strengths of academics lie in the realm of ideas that extend their current expertise to new intellectual and service frontiers. As lifelong learners, they work best with experience distilled as principles and guidelines that leave room for personal choice, individual creativity, and either collaborative or individual deliberation or reflection. These are paths best traveled with rich ideas, meaningful data, compelling narrative, and clear direction.

To take our experience a step farther, in working with academic learners we have found that principles and guidelines need to be measured in number, thoughtfully accessible, and immediately useful. We wrote this book to fill these needs, which in our opinion are not suitably attended to in the current literature but are very much on the minds of faculty, postdoctoral researchers, graduate students, and independent scholars with whom we have had the pleasure to work over the years.

Before we take up "Principles and Guidelines," we should provide a brief context for that discussion. This book takes a behavioral approach to developing successful research proposals. It depicts the process as it actually works itself out in most cases. In place of a strictly logical approach that starts and ends with the ordered sections of the grant proposal, we begin with the fact that doctoral candidates, postdoctoral students, and faculty researchers are all quite literally immersed in disciplines and their relevant literatures. Out of a welter of concepts, facts, and theories, we find ourselves proposing an idea that is the core of a research project. Our contention is that we should first develop that idea as fully as we can and infer directly from it all that we can.

The point is first to strengthen the idea in and of itself and all that follows from it easily and directly, including a sense of scale and timeline. Rather than proceed to writing the proposal, we instead conduct a review of the funding literature to determine in overview how others have developed a (somewhat) related project. From this review, we can readily gain a refined sense of scale, if not time and cost. Then and only then do we engage fully the several parts of a project proposal in which we refine the idea by relating it rigorously and systematically to prior research, applicable methods, necessary resources, and so on.

The chapters of this book follow this behavioral sequence as we address the three major constituencies of the higher-education research triumvirate: doctoral and postdoctoral students and research faculty. The more all three parties share a common basis for developing research proposals, the better the project will proceed and the better the outcomes will be.

Principles and Guidelines

The principles we have in mind are these:

- Quality proposals are compelling because they set out new ways to visualize and conceptualize an idea.
- To produce quality projects, we need to focus first and foremost on idea development and not on proposal development per se.
- Quality thinking supports compelling ideas; taken together, quality thinking and compelling ideas produce competitive submissions.

The guidelines are also few in number:

- First, learn and practice the repetitive nature of the art form we call *proposal development*. As you will see, the sections of a proposal visit and revisit ideas, starting with a very general exposition and making their way step-by-step to an altogether specific rendering of a proposal as a timeline/budget.
- Second, use verbal sketches to develop and move forward multiple idea and project alternatives.[1] We believe it is far easier to sketch and resketch an idea and its interconnections with the work of others—along with a series of proposed action steps—than it is to work initially with a fully developed text.
- Finally, learn to view ideas and evaluate your proposal from the funder's perspective. While an idea must first appeal to us and our colleagues, in the end, we must be able to view our idea from the vantage of others if we are to propose a project of more general or public interest.

We weave these principles and guidelines together in four of the chapters of this book: "Idea Development," "Funding," "Proposals," and "Managing a Funded Project."

Organization of This Book

In Chapter 2, we suggest ways to develop ideas in and of themselves and in relation to the art of crafting a proposal. For us, idea development is a flexible process that allows the lifelong academic learner to pave a path with sketches.

---

[1] Sketches tend to be written and can be as varied as vignettes, a draft letter to a close friend, or indeed any other creation that stimulates narrative or helps us break through writer's block. See *An Aside: The Nature of a Sketch* below.

In turn, the sketches allow the author of the ideas and the author's associates to parse core notions and develop project alternatives. Easily revised, the sketches allow for the restatement of ideas and implications with ease. With minimal effort, one can prepare several alternatives, analyze and assess their strengths and weaknesses, and then make an informed choice on which to develop into a proposal.

We begin this chapter with a discussion of ideas and their gestation as sketches. We introduce dimensions of inquiry to help clarify our thoughts and inform the writing of the proposal. We then move on to sketch meaningful idea/project alternatives—and their implications—so as to prepare for a thoughtful exchange with funders. By "thoughtful exchange" we mean the ability to discuss the purpose of the project, to demonstrate its relationship to other work (past and present), and to clearly and effectively articulate a scale of effort and length of time that makes a contribution to practice or understanding.

Importantly, sketches have range. You can sketch an idea; you can sketch related notions, pure or applied, larger or smaller in scale. You can sketch an approximation of the outcomes of your project in general and useful ways even at the start, along with its costs in terms of dollars and effort in orders of magnitude.

Sketches also boast an additive quality. In linking sketches to each other, you can easily, quickly, and with minimal effort move around the pieces and achieve great clarity and more defined rigor and precision. Moreover, in aligning sketches with each other, we are able to tease out the strands and implications that carry across our project to enhance its value and give it measured purpose. Rather than adduce these qualities from the start, we can begin to discern them as we note their recurrence across our sketches of the several aspects of a research project.

In the end, sketches yield fairly formed notions of what we are proposing, even without the details well worked out. More than an outline with dryly listed parts, a sketch provides a somewhat developed sense of an idea and a directional sense of related topics, methods, scale, time, and so on. As the sketches form up further in alignment with each other, discursive sentences flow freely and connected points take hold. In the end, the proposal elaborates the sketches in a narrative that begins with a casual tone and results in a statement so clear and compelling, it too can be viewed as a contribution to scholarship and knowledge.

The most important point is how we get from idea to proposal. Our route of travel is by way of segmented sketches leading to interconnected sketches leading ultimately to a proposal format that follows a semistandard document outline that encompasses a project's purpose, means, and outcomes. The completion of the process must be guided by management principles. These we sketch, too, in the last chapter.

This process takes time; indeed, quality takes time. That said, we firmly believe that the investment of time and effort in idea development is worthwhile. We have learned from experience that the only path to high-quality proposals and valued projects is through development of compelling ideas that fully engage funders. We believe the guidance presented in this book will make the intellectually intensive work of idea development more efficient, purposeful, productive, meaningful, and enjoyable.

The third chapter considers funding. In this section, we learn how to employ our sketches to conduct systematic searches of funding databases. We consider these databases an important form of "literature." We will take some time with the art of developing descriptors useful in searching large grant archives for matches with our interests. In terms of process, we will cast a relatively wide net in our initial search of funding databases. We seek first to understand what funders have supported that comes close (prima facie) to our interests. Subsequently we narrow our search and eliminate some early prospects as we gather additional information on a funder's program(s) of support. Finally, our database and other research will guide both our initial inquiry of a specific funder and our subsequent conversation or exchange with a program officer. At every turn, we will provide specifics based on the examples presented in Chapter 2, "Idea Development."

The fourth chapter turns to the writing of the proposal itself. Specifically, a principle presented earlier deserves fuller restatement here:

> Proposals are repetitive art forms in which each successive section revisits in greater detail the ideas presented in the first section of the proposal, where ideas are constructs built on our experiences and informed perceptions of the needs of others.

As we write the first section of the proposal document, it becomes altogether apparent how the ideas we present from the very start are the mainstays of all of the proposal's sections.

The initial statement of a *core idea* is a statement of purpose. This is key. The *restatement of ideas* in relationship to the context to which they will *contribute to knowledge or practice* renders the guiding ideas with greater specificity. The *actual work proposed* to realize the potential contribution of your ideas provides a more specific description, if you will, of a portrait of *ideas in action*. Then it is on to *staffing, timetable of activities,* and *budget* and *budget justification,* which show in greater detail how to implement your idea(s) as a project.

Chapter 5 discusses the nuances of managing a funded project. It presents in some detail all of the many roles the principal investigator/project director (PI/PD) plays as project CEO. From hiring staff to maintaining liaison with funders to becoming a resource for others on your topic of funded research, we work through all the 12 discrete roles of the PI/PD, as well as the excitement and responsibilities that accompany each role.

Overall, no project exists apart from its ideas, and no ideas exist apart from personal experience, curiosity, and a passion for inquiry. Moreover, there is no proposal apart from the alignment of ideas in more and even more detailed explications in successive proposal sections that involve a sound methodology, data analysis, and synthesis and evaluation.

The two of us know of nothing academic in nature that is more admirable than a powerful idea. Its implementation as a project and its dissemination as useful information or informed practice is an inspired contribution to organized fields of study, to the meaningful development of students and scholars, and to the voracious needs of a knowledge-based society that is increasingly becoming more global in nature, reach, and impact.

We trust that this book will help bring together connections between worthy ideas and the aspirations all of us have for furthering knowledge, sharing experience, and helping shape a better society and a more just world.

Arnold Shore and John Carfora

Autumn 2009

Acknowledgments

Anthropologists have long held that culture represents the sum total of everything social and physical in a society. In writing this book, we found that as authors we owe much to everybody and everything that helped us discover an engrossing topic and explore it in depth. For us, the list of those we need and want to acknowledge is so long—so much the sum total of all who have ever discussed idea and proposal development with us—that we will call out categories of contributors to our thinking followed by specific mention of those who helped guide the manuscript to completion.

Academic colleagues who worked with us to develop their research ideas and craft their research proposals allowed us entrée to their partially formed thoughts. From that necessarily unformed starting point, we learned together how to achieve conceptual clarity step-by-step. For the trust they placed in us and their openness to us, we thank them. We can only hope that we have repaid them all with a book that will truly help others with the formulation of research ideas into compelling research proposals.

In graduate proposal seminars and capstone courses where the requirement was to produce and defend a developed proposal, we learned from our students how to segment and sequence proposal development. Again, trust was critical. It is not easy for students to work on their vulnerable ideas with others. For their trust and their persistence—for their splendid proposals and heartfelt defenses in support of them—we thank all of these students with whom we worked so very closely and from whom we learned so very much.

As the illustrious social scientist Robert K. Merton famously observed, we stand on the shoulders of giants, as he did in writing an eponymous work on that very topic. We are not the first to treat the intellectual and practice dimensions of proposal writing. By paying attention to the very good work of others, we believe we have raised practice and discussion of proposal development to the next level. We hope, too, that someday another generation of academics will use our work to continue a fruitful conversation about research proposal development that should never end.

The manuscript benefited greatly from the encouragement and critique of others. We thank Mick Smyer, a delightfully intelligent colleague, for his enthusiasm for the project from the start. Mick is a researcher, writer, and editor whose early support for our work got us going and helped us stay the course. We thank, too, Tom Hoffmann for his detailed visual review of the manuscript. Tom's graphic design sensibility helped lay out text and table in what we believe is a welcoming format.

At SAGE Publications we owe much to Vicki Knight for her trenchant observations and advice and Sean Connelly for his deft parsing of what we were saying, and why. With kindness, firmness, and much intelligence, they helped produce a better book. We thank, too, the several reviewers of the book, including the following:

Pamela K. Terry
Western Illinois University

Marianne Hollis
Western Carolina University

Stephanie L. Carter Williams
University of Southern California

Robert Hard
University of Texas at San Antonio

Cris M. Sullivan
Michigan State University

Alma Gottlieb
University of Illinois at Urbana-Champaign

Kathleen J. Zavela Tyson
University of Northern Colorado

Denise Wallen
University of New Mexico

John V. Stone
Michigan State University

Page by page and chapter by chapter, they offered suggestions that made things clearer and more accessible. In thanking them, as in thanking all others, we take full personal responsibility for any and all remaining errors.

We close with sincere thanks to our families for all their support. They have heard tell of this book for the years it took to write it. They can now read it and see for themselves that the energy they lent us has now made it into print.

Arnold Shore

John Carfora

Spring 2009

About the Authors

Arnold R. Shore is currently Associate Vice Provost for Research at Boston College. He has headed two foundations—the Russell Sage Foundation and the Exxon Education Foundation—and has served on numerous nonprofit boards, including President, New York Regional Association of Grantmakers; Chair, Advisory Committee, Foreign Policy Association; and Member, National Commission on the Independent College (Council of Independent Colleges) and the Commission on International Education (American Council on Education). Arnold has taught at the University of Minnesota, Princeton University, Columbia University Teachers College, and Boston College. He received his PhD from Princeton University.

John M. Carfora is Executive Director for Research Advancement and Compliance at Loyola Marymount University in Los Angeles. An economist and recognized authority on research administration and international research collaborations, he has lectured at a number of colleges and universities throughout Europe, Canada, Africa, and the United States. He is Co-Chair of I-Group—a National Academy of Sciences committee on international research collaborations—as well as a member of the Board of Directors of the Immersive Education Initiative and a former member of the Board of Directors of the Alumni and Friends of the London School of Economics (1982–1990). He was a Fulbright Scholar to Ireland in 2009, was awarded the Distinguished Service Award from the National Council of University Research Administrators (www.ncura.edu) in 2007, and was an IREX Fellow to the former Soviet Union in the 1980s. He received his Ed.D. from the Department of Organization and Leadership at Teachers College, Columbia University.

1

Introduction

The Purpose of the Book

The purpose of this book is twofold. First, to help those seeking external funding to pursue high-quality initiatives by way of well-developed ideas expressed as fully developed project proposals. Second, to help those who have received funding successfully manage their projects with efficiency and effectiveness.

Let us unpack that a bit by way of three imperatives:

1. The endpoint is a successful proposal.

2. The starting point is an idea.

3. The point of connection between initiative and idea is the proposal.

What ties these points together is quality: The better developed the idea, the easier it is to more fully develop a proposal that anticipates, informs, and contributes to a quality project. Clearly, quality has its costs and benefits.

Costs are measured in time and effort, and indeed, it takes time-consuming reflection and dedicated effort to develop an idea and transform it into a thoughtful proposal and well-conceived project. Thank goodness, the benefits are substantial. In addition to making a more compelling case, a quality proposal based in a developed idea rewards its proponents with the level of clarity necessary for successful project implementation. In all, we believe that proposal development costs can be reduced and the benefits enhanced by following the guidance offered in this work.

It may be useful to take a second approach to unpacking the chapter's first sentence: The purpose of this book is to help those seeking external funding to pursue high-quality initiatives by way of well-developed ideas expressed as fully developed project proposals. To do so, we must unpack the logic of our approach.

The Logic of Our Approach

Our approach to the drafting of a research proposal—whether it is a dissertation or a National Institutes of Health (NIH) application—can be simply stated: *Achieve rigor in steps; achieve precision in stages.* We try to segment the process so the parts are manageable and the outcomes enjoyable and useful. We begin with an idea, then address funding, then turn to the writing of the proposal itself. The internal logic is to begin with what you care about and derive from it as much as you can. Once you have developed your idea in itself and all that flows from it, then and only then begin to take account of the resources, interests, and work of others.

For us, this first step toward implementing your idea should be to consider the resources and interests of funders who think programmatically about topics, and what they consider important and fundable may link in varying degrees to your interests. Their views of resources will help you scale—or rescale—your project. It follows for us that the last segment of our three-part approach is writing the proposal proper. One key section—the literature review—brings your idea right up against the work of others. At this point, with your developed idea in mind, you have already come to terms with one literature—the funding literature—and now you are better equipped to come to terms with the scholarly literature. Resource needs, alongside additional intellectual possibilities, may come from a deep dive into the academic work of others. Ideas that are yours from the start come from a wide array of sources, only some of which can be fully identified. You must ultimately turn to the professional literature if only to determine that your idea and the work you propose can be a contribution to knowledge.

You start with your idea. Focusing only on the idea, you produce sketches of

- the idea itself,
- what it can produce (knowledge, practice),
- a broad estimate of project costs,
- a first cut at project scale,
- a preliminary sense of project timeline.

Moving on to the funding literature, you focus on both on your idea and on the approaches, and resources of funders. Consider the following factors and write down your thoughts:

- What aspect(s) of your idea(s) are funders generally supporting?
- What may be necessary—what may be acceptable—to accommodate your idea to the approaches of the funding community?
- What changes may follow for what your idea can produce, both immediately and in the longer term?
- Taking account of order of magnitude, what changes in your initial estimates of project costs, scale, or timeline must you entertain?

Moving to the proposal, focus on your idea as strengthened by its encounter with the funding literature. You now search the academic literature and come to terms with it as you sketch the following sections of the semi-standard proposal format:

- *Core idea:* What you are proposing, why, with what benefits to practice or knowledge?
- *Context of your idea:* What is its relationship to the work of others (literature and other reviews)?
- *Methods:* How will you know?
- *Activities:* What will you do?
- *Products:* What will be the immediate outputs and longer-term outcomes?
- *Budget/timeline:* What costs (effort/dollars) over what periods of time?

To summarize, the logic of our approach is to start with one's idea and, in stages, move to take account of the approaches and work of others. Because we think of funding as an activity that collectively produces a literature and because it is in some ways easier to search that literature and come to terms with it, we make a review of funding prospects the second step. The last step is to take what we gained from idea development and the kinds of emphases the funding literature might introduce and pour the results into the semistandard categories one encounters in proposals. The core idea will carry over in the largest part. Costs, scale, and timeline might change. Taking account of intellectual context—by thoroughly reviewing the academic literature and professional work of others—will help infuse additional rigor into our thinking.

All told, the clearer we are about our core interests, our core idea, and what follows from it—and the more we understand about the funding and intellectual contexts and traditions in which our idea resides—then the more honestly and usefully adaptive and flexible we can be in pursuing our proposed work in a rigorous and precise academic fashion.

It is worth repeating that the target audiences of this book are doctoral and postdoctoral students and research faculty. All three need to share a deep appreciation of a workable approach to proposal development and project management if (a) a doctoral student's dissertation or postdoctoral student's research application is to succeed easily and fruitfully with advisers' help or (b) a faculty researcher's project is to succeed with graduate and/or postdoctoral assistance.

Demystifying Proposal Development

We seek to demystify the proposal development process by maintaining a steadfast focus on a well-developed idea as the starting point for a fully developed proposal and project. Standard proposal advice begins with the requirements of the proposal and a clear understanding of the funder's guidelines. We insist that the first steps taken toward a fully developed project proposal starts with an idea and its exploration.

In an idea reside linkages with past work and connections with useful and desirable outcomes. Only with a well-developed idea in hand can we make the highest and best use of the discipline and structure of the proposal to fully elaborate the idea as an initiative that can be implemented in a reasonable period of time with sensible expenditure of funds and effort.

We present methods for developing an idea that are straightforward. We employ verbal sketches to help you learn what you truly think before linking your idea to a funder's interest. With your sketches in hand, you are in a position to know early on whether your interests and those of funders intersect or whether you are twisting yourself into pretzel shapes in the hope of gaining financial support.

An Aside   The Nature of a Sketch

A sketch captures in broad strokes the essence of a topic. It is purposely incomplete yet substantial enough to yield the shape and form of an idea. It proceeds with a story told in a casual way about the origin of an idea. The result is a nugget or two around which we can build a more complete story line and from which we can derive implications for other aspects of a proposal, which we can also sketch.

For those who encounter difficulties with writing—or, more precisely, trouble beginning to write or trouble sustaining a written piece—a sketch is a way to express thoughts as statements that make general sense. For those who insist on outlining an idea, a sketch can be viewed as an incomplete description that focuses on up to three major dimensions or considerations and begins to fill in some detail under each. While not a full outline, a sketch yields a proto-outline, or a way of putting forth some tentative notions that are, to begin with, partially described and easily altered. Our basic point—stated elsewhere and repeated here—is that we pursue rigor in steps and precision in stages. For most all of us, there is an innate ability to work better with a partially complete statement in hand rather than try to fill in all the details from the start.

As you make your way through this book, you will find that we present sketches of ideas and other project elements, including products, scale, cost, timeline, and so on. Because sketches are pliable, we can inflect them with applied and pure characteristics as well as by a larger or smaller scale. These are two ways in which a sketch, because it is easily altered and because it seeks rigor and precision over time, aids in the always necessary reformulation of ideas. We can entertain alternatives systematically as we pursue the formulation and definition of a project to which we will dedicate considerable thought, time, and effort in its execution and completion.

The Key Role of Ideas

In emphasizing the idea as the starting point, this book does intersect some with the extant literature on proposal development. We agree that you need to establish both your idea and its context. We concur that you need to pay attention to presenting your idea in the required format. However, we begin to diverge from conventional wisdom when we emphasize the need to start with your major strength—your good idea—and drive that idea toward implementation in proposal sections that are progressively more detailed. The idea you start with gets visited and revisited from a number of vantages, all in an effort to develop and elaborate context and methods, timetable, and costs. In this process, both the proposer of the idea and the idea itself mature.

To be fair, in emphasizing ideas, this book finds itself taking exception to some of the conventional wisdom offered in the literature. An overwhelming number of works on proposal development write to the lowest common denominator by attempting to develop the proposal, not the person and ideas. We do not believe that it is useful to simply say to proposal developers, "Be specific!" To fully develop your idea, you need to be general and encompassing, self-aware and cognizant of the work of others, attentive to project choices and alternatives, and mindful of both generally and specifically required resources to launch a successful initiative. Each proposal topic requires appropriate treatment. You will need to be clear both generally and specifically at several levels of abstraction if the funder is to understand your project's progression from rounded idea to budgeted and evaluated effort.

All of the following need clarity as individual proposal sections and, overall, as an integrated initiative:

- The essence of your idea and its intellectual, academic, and/or applied contexts
- The idea made more specific and palpable in the outlined description of methods and proposed activities
- The idea revisited from the vantage of staffing and other budgetary and program-related needs

The principles and guidelines we offer in Chapter 2 (Ideas) and in Chapter 4 (Proposals) will make these points real and readily attainable. The guidelines we present in Chapter 3 (Funding) will help make our ideas and our proposed projects a reality. The guidelines we present in Chapter 5 (Managing a Funded Project) will help your idea produce successful outputs and outcomes.[1] Funding starts with an idea; thus we turn to Idea Development in Chapter 2.

---

[1] While the terms *outputs* and *outcomes* are unnecessarily clunky and arid, they are terms that are widely used and accepted in evaluation practice, which is precisely why we use them in this book.

2

Idea Development

The Purposes of Ideas

In the world of project and program proposals, an idea makes a novel and useful connection between significant need and purposeful action. A proposal's core idea also guides the structured use of scarce resources (talent, knowledge, money) toward making a connection between need and action that is both real and of benefit to many. In all, an idea is a project's foundational starting point. As such, it serves several key purposes:

The idea is the fundamental source of a project's contribution. A project is worthwhile when it makes a contribution to knowledge, scholarship, creative activity, informed practice, social justice, the general welfare, or some other high purpose. It is an idea that captures and formulates the potential contribution and guides us toward its realization. With idea-inspired creativity, captured in clear language and guided by appropriate structure, a future possibility feels real and palpable here and now to both its author(s) and potential supporter(s).

The idea is the fundamental source of proposal and project excitement. Nothing quite excites like an idea that grips the imagination with a sense of insight and purpose. The enthusiasm an idea generates is not peripheral. It is central to persuading others that our proposal is workable and worthwhile. We can indeed get excited about something that does not yet exist if it is part of a larger and longer process of idea development that promises, if not ensures, a mature and reasoned outcome.

The enduring insight and purpose of an idea help sustain staff interest and commitment over the course of a project. Things do become more fluid once we begin implementing a project. The strength and vitality of the idea remind us of the high purposes we are pursuing and readily bring us back—with inspiration, passion, and a renewed commitment—to the formulation that guided us from the outset.

Clearly, a solid idea is integral to the development of a worthwhile and successful proposal initiative; because of our idea, a project endeavor becomes grantworthy. Where do such ideas come from? How do we gestate them? We believe they come from taking time and sharing joy in their development.

Idea Gestation

To produce an idea that can contribute to furthering knowledge, producing useful excitement, and sustaining staff effort requires several essential components, including the following: (1) interplay, (2) support, (3) structure, (4) sketches, and (5) critiques, deconstruction and reflection. Let's see how these various segments intertwine.

To develop a project idea requires the interplay of conversation and consideration where both contribute to strengthening the idea's clarity, connections, and reach. This cannot be forced. Through interplay, ideas and passions make their way back and forth among trusted and interested colleagues in what the German existentialist Martin Heidegger termed the *mitdasein*—the existence between and among ideas and us. In this truly shared context, ideas begin to come into focus and take shape and form as an understandable, intelligent, and collective effort as we relate to each other and to this notion—this idea—that is partnering with us.

Individual perspectives oriented to a common idea begin to develop support and structure for exploring an idea's positive and promising aspects. Interplay sets the tone, while interaction produces structure. In turn, structure produces support. In the multistep relationship between idea and support, we should enjoy the give-and-take that produces clarity and élan.

In developing the idea and strengthening it to the point where it can benefit from critique and assessment, the authors fully recognize and appreciate that precision is a managed variable. At first, we are rather easy about the development of the idea. Only after interplay, support, and structure have strengthened a wisp of a notion into a fairly robust idea should we introduce the precision and rigor of critique, deconstruction, and reflection. Putting tough questions to an idea before its time will invariably impede progress. Never putting a developed idea to the test will assuredly produce failure. With interplay, support, and structure as the foundation, critique takes us to a place where the idea is not just ours alone, but potentially much more widely shared with others.

It is important to note that some parts of an idea are best worked out individually—some in collaboration with others. Some parts are best worked out in writing, some in editing, and some in affable and reflective interaction. There is almost a natural division of labor based on strengths of individuals interacting through collaboration. That said, not all researchers prefer working in collaborative groups, so what if you prefer working on your own? We have found that even in those cases where researchers prefer working alone, they need to seek the advice, expertise, and opinion of valued colleagues and close friends. Others should serve as peer reviewers who can offer—at various levels—trusted insight and meaningful perspective.

What gets us where we are going in good stead are written sketches. We begin by sketching the *idea*. Second, we sketch *outputs and outcomes embedded in the idea*. Third, we sketch, or estimate, *costs* and demands on those engaged in the proposed project. When we have all three sketches in hand—idea, outputs and outcomes, cost—we are in a solid position to elaborate the idea further by the fourth step: using the discipline of a sketched-in *timeline, budget, and budget justification*. Following this fourth step we go on to the last step: *Writing an abstract* that elegantly summarizes our idea, its deliverables, the costs and benefits, and the nature and scale of the project we propose.

An Aside

In our description of the roles of interplay, support, and structure in the initial development and exploration of an idea, we are drawing on our personal experience of working with colleagues on developing successful proposal ideas. The atmosphere is light; the banter, caring. Notions catch fire, and we all take pleasure in the steps we have taken together toward clarity. As one of us introduces a possible connection no one may have thought about before, the atmosphere sometimes gets almost euphoric and often quite passionate. We are trekking into unknown territory, and we are getting somewhere with pleasure, if not joy. Having an old hand guide the conversation can facilitate the exchange, but that is not altogether necessary if colleagues go into the initial conversation knowing their individual contributions to the interplay will—even without trying all that hard or worrying about being "graded" by others—result in a better idea, a compelling proposal, and a better project.

As we now turn below to the five-part process previously outlined, we have opted to present a different example to illustrate each type of sketch we employ in developing a notion into a rounded idea. Rather than attempt to find one all-encompassing example, we present several ideas, each chosen to illustrate a single dimension of the overall idea development process. Looking ahead, when we turn to the development of the full proposal (last section of this book), we follow a single example through all the stages of proposal development.

Written Sketches

1. SKETCHING AN IDEA

A good example has great value. All of ours are based on our experiences and ideas and represent the products of shared idea development. We offer the sketch of an idea so you will have a firm sense of what we have in mind. We also offer variations on the idea (and, later on, variations on all the sketches provided). The idea is not only to summarize our thoughts succinctly but also to put them in a form in which we can easily work with these thoughts, as well as change and revise them with ease.

Idea Sketch 1

A librarian was seeking support for an archive. After some flowing conversation, it started to become clear that while she would love to have general support for running and maintaining the archive, her real passion was to use the archive to teach history. Asked to describe how she would propose to teach an archive-based history course, the sketch of the idea took form.

Students would read the same short archival document and parse its meaning. They would read two additional archival documents, one written a little before the foundational document and one a little after. The students would ask themselves the question: Do I still interpret the meaning of the original document the way I did initially? Students would venture a little further backward and forward in time until the meaning of the foundational document did not change much with additional historical comparisons.

In Idea Sketch 1, we should note that the paragraph sketch is rather short and to the point. It resulted from a conversation that elicited an impassioned and quite smart notion of how one might teach history. From this example, we should take heart that while clarity and simplicity are sometimes hard to achieve, colleagues working together on a notion in progress are apt to find themselves successful to the core: We can grab hold of an idea in a supportive environment and commit it to writing all in a relatively short space of time.

Because we are working with sketches, it is also rather easy to try on alternatives. For example, with the original sketch in hand, the librarian-teacher could easily develop a variant on the archival-based teaching of history by concentrating on a particular subject—say, Latin American history—and link the study of history to the acquisition of usable language skills. She could also try on the notion of developing more specialized techniques or general guidelines for the archival-based study of historical personages as over and against historical events or issues. Finally, she could also try further developing the approach by engaging teachers on the one hand and archivists on the other in a common training program to learn more about the different strengths each brings to this highly promising approach to teaching history.

In all, our sketch is easily transportable and easily inflected—two characteristics that make it ideal for the gestation stage of idea development.

Knowledge-Oriented Alternatives

Above, we presented *practice*-oriented alternatives. Knowledge-oriented alternatives abound.

The librarian's idea could turn in the direction of what students learn employing the archival-based approach described as over and against a much broader use of sources and materials. Are conclusions similar? Are certain historical topics—sequencing, figures, events—more or less emphasized?

This idea could embody an interesting pedagogical methodology formulated to make a contribution to historiography, or how we come to know history. One could assign some students to the archival class and others to standard classes on the same semester-long topic. In assessing differences in emphases and conclusions, the two classes could come together for a topic-based discussion that also speaks directly to the inclusions and omissions of differing modes of historical inquiry. Let's put the matter into a brief sketch:

In casual conversation, two history teachers realized that while they shared a passion for teaching 20th-century American history, they differed sharply in the degree to which their classes made use of archival materials. One of the teachers tended to tie everything into original source documents ordered carefully by time. The other would ask students to pursue themes—the rise of populism, the role of political parties, the unfolding nature of the corporation—to whatever sources the students chose to use.

Inspired by their exchange, the two teachers decided to teach two course sections in two very different ways. Since an archive on campus had an extensive collection of the writings of several populist figures, they decided to offer Populist Thought in America in the 19th century. One section would use only the archival approach described earlier. The other would use eclectic sources, including the Internet. Toward the end of the course, students would present their papers to their respective classes. In the final week of the course, the instructors would introduce historiographical matters, including choice of problems, nature of conclusions, and depth and breadth of historical understanding. Together, the instructors would systematically review student papers and student presentations and discussion. The instructors would then produce a pedagogical paper designed to sensitize other faculty in other schools to their findings and the mini-experiments they might themselves conduct by employing a coordinated teaching approach.

To the outcomes embedded in the idea we now turn.

2. SKETCHING THE EXPECTED OUTPUTS OF AN IDEA

With a sketch of an idea in hand, it is not difficult to derive embedded outputs. That is to say, in the case of Idea Sketch 1, it is possible to develop a course of study for undergraduate or graduate students that makes good use of an archive in a course that burrows deep into its subject matter. To further elaborate this point, let us take another idea that led almost immediately to a set of outputs that began to define a workable project.

Idea Sketch 2

A number of research librarians and library organizations became concerned about the deterioration of books published after 1850, a watershed date that demarcates a switch from printing books on rag stock to printing books on acid-based paper manufactured from wood pulp. Discussion led in several directions. One could conduct research on the nature of acid (and alkaline) papers to understand more fully the chemical/physical basis of book deterioration. One could look to temperature and humidity controls to slow deterioration. One could capture content and transfer it to another medium (fiche, digital disk, etc.). The third possibility seemed especially promising. An idea and its outputs began to clarify when several proponents of preservation realized that all preservation media have finite life spans. A series of connections followed, and an idea characterized by its outputs began to take shape.

A thinking factory could track technology developments by transferring and retransferring content from one preservation medium to another as technologies are developed that are longer-lived, less costly, and/or more reliable. By providing content transfer services at a sizable scale, cost could be driven down and larger numbers of research libraries could avail themselves of high-quality, thoughtful preservation services. The capacity of the proposed center would allow it to address large, vulnerable collections of printed scholarship. By establishing the factory as a nonprofit corporation, one could help ensure that funds would be regularly invested in research and development.

To be clear, there are both outputs and outcomes embedded in our example. The first are necessary to realize the second. In this case, the output is the thinking factory; the outcome is the preservation of books and manuscripts. Both outputs and outcomes should be clearly distinguished for the sake of the project and the sake of the funder. For the principal investigator (PI), the outputs will take up most all of the project effort. For the funder, the effects of the outputs—that is, the outcomes—will be of greatest interest and will vie for the attention of the PI. These directly address the high purposes, or programmatic interests, of the sponsoring agency. Of course, there should be a proximate and necessary relationship between the two so that what the project does can ultimately realize great effect.

Outputs allow us to surround an idea with additional structure that further develops its strengths, answers critical questions, and adds essential depth and breadth. The outputs should be described with as much detail as is useful in a first blush attempt to say where the idea is taking us. In Idea Sketch 2, we have provided enough information on outputs to know that the idea we have in mind is highly innovative (a thinking factory), which in this case is large in scale, very much dependent on staying abreast of research and development, and clearly related to the high purpose of library archival preservation. In presenting this output, we are working with the funder to help assess and evaluate the project we propose. It is our feeling that both outputs and outcomes should be specified and, as we shall see below, developed in detail by way of a timeline, or expected dates for their realization.

Just a few sentences will show us where we are heading and why. As in the case of sketching the initial idea, we have a format in which we can easily entertain variations on a theme. For example, the proponents of the thinking factory could develop a joint proposal with a business school to work out a business plan for an enterprise that would be self-sustaining in a relatively few years while generating adequate surplus (there is no profit in the nonprofit world) to maintain a keen research and development (R&D) edge. Another variation on the theme is a breakout of the types of books and other printed materials that would work best with one or another preservation approach. The project could spend useful time and effort determining its best chances for success and then test those notions in initial experimenting forays. Finally, a third variation would begin with a number of higher education/library institutions to ensure sufficient demand to warrant bringing a full-scale thinking factory on line. This alternative anticipates a topic we will turn to in short order.

Science of Preservation

In pursuing other alternatives, we could focus on the science of preservation. This interest could range from the microscopic study of fibers that make up paper and cloth to the transfer of content from one preservation medium to another. The casual, almost conversational tone of a sketch could help get down the main idea (and later, its implications) instead of getting knotted in details from the start. Let's start this sketch and leave its completion to you the reader.

> A student of information science took note that work was already progressing at a considerable scale on digitizing library holdings in the United States and elsewhere. She made a quick assumption that while some would conclude that digitized content would truly endure forever, others would wonder about the stability of digitally encoded books, pamphlets, ephemera, and so on. Depending on the nature and form of the digital record, what level of accuracy could one expect over what periods of time? How could the effective lifetime of a digital format be enhanced? How easily could existing digital formats be transferred to new or emerging ones? Indeed, do some material science principles exist that would determine the ability to link digital preservation approaches to each other and thus extend the lifetimes of content across a number of digital media?
>
> On reflection, the student found herself drawn to a combination of approaches:
>
> - Study of successful digital format linkages to date
> - Current and prospective range of digital memory devices
> - Theoretical possibilities taking account of demand for storage based on a publication explosion approaching an exponential curve
>
> The student, excited by a study that crossed historical data and material science both experimentally and theoretically, proceeds to think about the implications of this work and the scale and timeline that would help form a viable and useful study.

Your imaginations, outlooks, and capabilities will carry you in directions of great interest to you and other reflective scholars. We urge once again that you the researcher view sketches as comfortable ways to begin to take on a problem that may well blossom into an exciting proposal and a well-executed project.

With a brief sketch of the idea in hand and with a brief statement of embedded outcomes at the ready, we can sketch in cost. Let's turn to that topic now.

3. SKETCHING COST

To further structure our idea in a preliminary way, we turn to estimating cost. In our sketching mode, we are trying our hand at producing order-of-magnitude estimates, or approximations, as to what it will cost to realize the ideas we have roughed in. Thinking of the cost estimates as handy guides for some aspects of project decision making will be useful. For example, cost estimates help us decide about the scale at which we will pursue our project: the number of people we might involve, the number of alternatives we might pursue, the length of time needed to conduct the project, the ways we will assess and synthesize findings, and the ways we will disseminate what we have learned from inquiry.

In our experience, the joint discussion of outputs, outcomes, and costs can be as valuable as the initial discussion of the idea alone. In our search for traction to get our idea launched, cost determination is a flexible discipline for helping us understand how much we can do, with what resources, and in what period of time. We can scale our costs to budgetary guidelines (usually, but not always, with a sense of constraint), or we can entertain a robust budget that fully supports all the outcomes we would like to realize. Just achieving some focus—though not an altogether clear focus at first—on the relationship of costs and outputs/outcomes allows us to understand how ambitious we want to be, how realistic we think we ought to be, and how to find a midpoint that realistically appears optimal.

Idea Sketch 3

A professor was seeking a way to help good ideas travel from one K–12 teacher to others. A distinction he drew between *idea originators* on the one hand and *idea subscribers* (adopters and adaptors) on the other helped the idea take flight. The former are those who dream up teaching geometry through the construction of geodesic domes, or teaching language arts by establishing a school radio station, or teaching art to special education students by having them design T-shirts which they silkscreen with their art. The latter—*idea* subscribers—are dedicated teachers who know how to make good use of meaningful ideas in their classrooms; in effect they are practitioners who can adapt ideas and visions to a range of student learners.

(Continued)

(Continued)

The professor simultaneously further developed the idea and made it possible to estimate cost and scale by considering ways to organize support for the idea originators on the one hand and the idea subscribers on the other.

Based on experience, the professor knew idea originators in public school systems would continue to dream up good ideas without dollar support but would benefit greatly from peer recognition. Drawing on just such experience, he recognized that it would be necessary to support idea subscribers (both adopters and adapters) with small grants to aid their implementation of new classroom ideas. Experience also taught that teachers working in relative isolation of each other could recognize and benefit from the ideas of colleagues and would more readily seek funds if the application was simple (one page) and turnaround fast (several days).

With the cost of small grants to idea subscribers placed between $100 and $300 each, the cost of a recognition ceremony estimated at $2,000 to $3,000, and the cost of minimum adequate administrative capacity estimated at $80,000 a year, one could scale resources to the nature of the locale served (contiguous or separated school districts, and public and private school partnerships) and the numbers and types of supporting activities (catalogs presenting ideas, as well as biographical sketches of idea originators and idea subscribers, numbers of award ceremonies for originators, television coverage of new classroom ideas in action, and so on). Mixing and matching attainable outcomes and their costs to a series of processes of reasonable and manageable scale, the project proponents were ready to land on a feasible alternative as a starting point for further discussion.

Alternative Cost Sketch

Rather than focus on cost directly, we might do so more indirectly and more personally by narrowing in on those who originate projects and those who adopt and adapt them. We might look at the motivations and teaching styles by focusing on the presence or absence of networks among teachers and the role of leadership (by teachers, master teachers, principals, and superintendents). We might, therefore, in addition to our usual project-related concerns about cost ask ourselves about the nature of intrinsic or nonmonetary rewards that lead to origination or subscription by teachers. The cost of doing a project—plays a helpful part in guiding effort, we shall see—but nonmonetary rewards can also push us in the direction of a very interesting alternative sketch.

For example, a new superintendent was brought in to head a large urban school system. Experienced in the positions, if not the arguments about what makes the greatest difference in student learning, she had long ago landed on her three choices: involvement of parents in the education of their children, full engagement of teachers in the classroom and the wider school environment, and useful administrative support. The superintendent knew there were outstanding teachers whose students were learning well by any number of measures (e.g., high classroom grades, outstanding standardized test scores, and extensive involvement with schoolwide activities). She also knew that these teachers drew great pleasure and personal reward from working with colleagues. She surmised that the teachers she chose would be ready to work with others to achieve a higher and perhaps broader level of success within the schools and across the district.

The superintendent approached two self-motivated teachers from each of seven schools to organize an idea originator/idea subscription approach to highlighting and disseminating teaching that worked well for students. The teachers, having listened to the superintendent's sketch of her idea, decided to augment the model in a critical way: They would include parents from the start to engage community interest and enthusiasm for successful teaching approaches that could be practiced in the school and in the home. Their enthusiasm for working with others went beyond the bounds the superintendent originally set. The result was stunning.

Having read this far, you can appreciate that getting started on an idea can be made easier and more enjoyable where sketches are employed. The more natural sound of the sketched idea encourages us to write down our thoughts in a compact and logical fashion. While our imaginations fire, we know that our critical capacities can hold sway soon. After the sketched-in notion takes form, we can strengthen it both with creativity and analysis and do so readily. Even if the sketch goes on, it never reaches the length of a chapter and therefore serves up a wieldy format for revision, responsible tinkering, reinterpretation, and realignment.

A Budgetary Aside

The K–12 example presented above is based on an actual funded project. On the face of things, the cost figures are all wrong or at least out of balance. The largest portion of funds is devoted to administration, the smallest to the grants themselves. And the amount devoted to recognition seems out of balance with both individual grant costs and the overall costs of administration. In actuality, a support structure capable of eliciting and reviewing large numbers of small grants is expensive. Moreover, the number of small grants can become rather large, and derivative activities—such as providing catalogue descriptions to very large numbers of teachers—can be extremely demanding even of professional administrators with considerable firsthand experience in the classroom.

As we have seen, sketches easily allow for the development of alternatives. For example, one possibility was to conduct the aforementioned project in both a private school system and a public school system. This option would allow us to gauge from the outset just how valuable our idea is as well as how attractive it might be in practice. The project could also entertain making grants at only the $100 level to keep variable costs to a minimum. The kinds of projects it attracts and the value they produce would be of great interest in a scarce funding environment. Finally, the project could set up a direct comparison of programmatic versions that work within a single small district with those working across districts or in very large district settings.

Our sketches keep the process light, enjoyable, and productive. We have not invested a great deal of time in them. As we have seen, they are brief and easily altered. Because sketches are so flexible and manageable, we can try out several formulations, or variations on the idea, that may have different starting points or differing emphases. With very little baggage—sketches of the idea, outcomes, and order-of-magnitude cost estimates—we can guide ourselves to the next stage, that of idea elaboration.

4. IDEA ELABORATION

The next step is to elaborate the idea more fully. As we do so, we begin to address the process of presenting a project's interconnected parts to a broader public and ultimately to a funder.

We have in hand our *idea* and its *outputs* roughly budgeted to what we might term a *working sense of scale*. Everything we have done so far flows from the idea we have developed. We want to continue in this vein as we further elaborate both the idea and the budget. The approach that works best for us is to develop a *timeline of activities* that links the idea to its *outputs* in more specific ways. As you will see, we will find ourselves developing a checklist of activities that also serves as *a checklist of cost items*. This checklist will help us reflect further upon the idea itself and on the budget we are forming.

We have found it easier to reason backward from outcomes to specific project activities than to specify activities and reason forward to their outcomes. Looking forward with clarity is daunting. Looking backward from future outcomes to necessary project activities seems to be something we humans do more naturally. In his book, *Studies in Ethnomethodology*, Harold Garfunkel (1991) argues that people plan from the present back to the past. In the world as he sees it, looking forward (planning) hardly ever occurs. In its place, people project forward what they have experienced in retrospect. Working with a technique called "futures history"—essentially a technique that invites us to look forward 10 to 15 years to plan the future of an organization—facilitators have generally found it best to start with the future and imagine how we got there. In effect, they are taking Garfunkel's insight about the power of retrospective thinking and tricking it into thinking about the future in a backward-looking way.

Project structure, a necessity for constructing an orderly presentation and greater plausibility for a project, builds easily and readily on itself. We can employ a timeline to help develop a sense of order in our proposed activities. For example, looking backward from the successful conduct of a project,

- we can specify the order of activities we followed to get them into a rough timeline;
- we can specify the emphasis we placed on certain activities to give us a sense of what has priority and at what time;
- we can look at the interrelationship among activities to detect overlap (purposeful or accidental) and complementarity (coming at the same task in a number of ways);
- we can reconsider the coordination of activities to determine if administrative needs are in consonance with the timeline we see beginning to take shape or whether we need to add in administrative desiderata to arrive at a workable timeline.

To take the K–12 educational innovation sketch a step farther, we might develop the following timeline for a 3-year project. How, in retrospect, we reach the end of the project will help us determine how to get there.

Figure 2.1   Sample Timeline

	Year 1				Year 2				Year 3			
	1st Qtr	2nd Qtr	3rd Qtr	4th Qtr	1st Qtr	2nd Qtr	3rd Qtr	4th Qtr	1st Qtr	2nd Qtr	3rd Qtr	4th Qtr
Hire Director	▬											
Hire Staff		▬▬										
Develop Grant Guidelines	▪		▬									
Process Grant Applications					▬			▬▬		▬▬		
Announce Awards					▪			▪				▪
Refine Program Guidelines					▬▬							
Hold Award Ceremony					▬				▬			▬
Develop Catalog				▬▬					▬▬			
Report to Funder(s)				▪					▪			▪

Even in its first draft, our timeline is instructive. We are on a fast track. Expeditiously we need to hire a director and staff who are advocates for innovation in teaching and are able to administer the program on a day-to-day basis while popularizing it and disseminating its products. We need to formulate guidelines for the program, publicly announce a "Call for Proposals," process grant applications, make and announce awards, and refine our program with the help of evaluators—all approximately within a year.

There is heavy overlap of activities during the start-up period. We are simultaneously hiring staff, developing the grant process, and making choices about participating districts. We have found a complementary, time-related way to emphasize grant awards alongside celebrations of teacher innovations.

Understanding more fully how we might implement our idea actually helps elaborate the idea (the core of our work has a lot to do with teacher and administrator presentations in person and in written form) and more accurately estimate the cost of the effort (the number of districts and the number of participating teachers, or awardees, will enable us to get a handle on the variable costs in the budget).

5. DEVELOPING THE PROJECT ABSTRACT AND REFLECTING ON OUR WORK

Maybe the hardest thing to produce in first draft is the abstract, an elegant summary that takes us to the heart of the project in few words but with sufficient detail to make and hopefully advance a compelling and interesting case. We like to sketch it at the very beginning, read it regularly, and revise it constantly. We write it one final time when we have in hand sketches of the idea, timeline, and budget that have been actively related to each other. These ingredients help us finally revise the abstract by aligning it fully with the idea, adding brief descriptions of major outcomes, and providing the reader—the funder—with a rough sense of overall cost and time to completion from the very start. Indeed, it may be useful to think of the abstract as a working "30-second elevator speech" that researchers are always asked for. It is not just an idea, but an idea made manifest by a timeline and budgetary details.

Chapter Summary

In our approach to developing research ideas, precision is a variable, not a constant. We begin by sketching a project idea and then, in steps and stages, develop more precisely what we have in mind. The process we advocate extends the idea by sketching its implications for cost, scale, outcomes, and timeline. Step-by-step, the idea takes on a more robust form as we explore it and what follows directly from it. As we enter a second stage—as we begin to take account of the interest of funders (what we term funder-based search literature) and the intellectual context and traditions in which the idea resides (empirically based scholarly literature)—we can also progress in an orderly way toward greater precision and rigor.

Stepping back just a bit, we emphasized in this chapter how to get started on a research project that could range as widely as a dissertation or a competitive proposal (for funding) to a foundation or federal agency. An undifferentiated task is almost always overwhelming. A task with discernible, manageable parts invites engagement. Moreover, in getting started on formulating an idea and exploring what flows from it, we also emphasized the utility of trying out alternatives in an efficient way.

Hardly ever, if at all, does a project idea proceed in a straight line from initial concept, to developed proposal, and on to a completed project. Our approach to the development of research ideas presents a way to get things started comfortably, to explore implications thoughtfully, and to introduce alternatives efficiently and effectively.

REFLECTIVE QUESTIONS

The questions we ask you to reflect on presume that you have made good progress in sketching your idea and all that flows directly from it: order of magnitude cost and scale, products (outputs and outcomes), and timeline. The reflective questions we pose are designed to begin to introduce greater precision and rigor into these components of your developing project. Here, as elsewhere, we suggest you take things one step at a time. You can always ask hard and tough questions. We sometimes refer to these as the "easy hard questions" since they are simple to formulate and almost impossible to respond to fully. For example: *Just what do you mean by X, or Y, or Z?* Or, *Are you being naive to believe your project will be completed on time and within the costs you estimate?* And so on. Here we would offer questions designed to strengthen your sketches rather than bearing down on questions that we believe prematurely seek exquisite levels of precision and rigor:

1. In thinking about your core idea, does it address a need that has been assessed or measured objectively, or does it derive from a personal or subjective perception?

There is no right answer. Sometimes we start where the work of others leaves off. Sometimes we begin with a hunch. Reflecting on the nature of the idea and its origin will help you begin to strengthen it from the start.

2. Have you considered the individual and organizational assets that might contribute to the development of your core idea or that help you better reflect on estimates and descriptions of costs, scale, timeline, and products?

Sometimes we overlook useful resources close at hand. They may be resident in other departments or outside the college or university. They may be acquaintances or friends. By extending our networks to include a wider range of academic and nonacademic resources, we can access points of view that are helpful to us in reflecting on our first approximations, our starting points, and our overall direction.

3. Are the activities you enumerate initially sufficiently detailed and reasonably ordered to begin connecting the idea sketches and sketches of outcomes?

It is not sufficient to pose purely logical connections. We need to try, even early on, to offer connections that make sense both in terms of rationale (linking ideas to outcomes) and operations (conducting the project in an efficient and effective manner). Here we wish to note that we are beginning to think about aligning interconnected efforts with each other. This helps make the most compelling case for undertaking a project and doing it well.

4. Does the project complement or reside in a larger programmatic effort?

No matter how encompassing a project may seem to us—to an academic adviser or a funder—it is usually viewed as part of something larger. Looking ahead to the next chapter, we may find the funding literature useful in beginning to see how our effort relates programmatically to the efforts of others. Similarly, we need to place our work in an intellectual context that is larger and more encompassing than the ideas we are pursuing.

Figure 2.2, a diagram of our conceptual framework, will help guide your reading of the rest of this book as we move from the development of ideas to the review of the funding literature and then on to the development of a compelling proposal.

Figure 2.2   Conceptual Framework: From Idea to Outline and Proposal

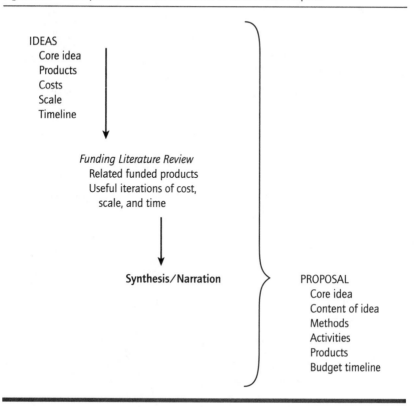

IDEAS
   Core idea
   Products
   Costs
   Scale
   Timeline

Funding Literature Review
   Related funded products
   Useful iterations of cost,
     scale, and time

Synthesis/Narration

PROPOSAL
   Core idea
   Content of idea
   Methods
   Activities
   Products
   Budget timeline

3

Funding

In principle, the search for funding starts with your interests supported by your vision of an optimal project. In practice, it starts with the sketches of your project that we developed in Chapter 1. The wellspring of your funding request is your core idea sketched as a purposeful project that advances knowledge or practice in a thoughtful and structured way.

With the sketches of your idea and its project outcomes, project budget, and timeline, your search for funding continues with your efforts to find a solid and substantive match between your interests and those of a funder. Your sketches are of great value in finding a topical match. The sketches can also provide guidance in sifting the information you will encounter on what we will term a *funder's secondary purposes*, which include such matters as a funder's interest in employing grants organized around a substantive topic (say, health, education, or science) to simultaneously help build institutions, develop a successor generation of project/program professionals, or guide or reform the agenda for a field of inquiry or practice. Your core idea and its sketch-based elaboration help you understand from the outset how encompassing your project can be while still focusing on your chosen purposes.

Be clear that you are not chasing funding possibilities; rather, you are thoughtfully seeking a match on two levels—topical interest and secondary funding goals. Appreciate from the start that these matches are not always precise. What you seek is the best information you can find on both primary interests and secondary goals that will help you make your proposal responsive to a funder's programmatic guidelines.

Describing Your Project

To start building the connection between your interests and those of a funder, we want to derive from our sketches a number of ways to characterize, or describe our purposes. This exercise allows us to spread a wider net for identifying funding sources. To provide specific examples, we will revisit three of the idea sketches we presented in the first chapter and characterize each in five differing ways.

You will recall that we presented a project on the use of an archive to teach history (Idea Sketch 1). We will use descriptors to characterize this project in the following ways:

- Teaching technique for history
- Teaching use of an archive
- In-depth pedagogical approach
- Community-oriented study of history
- Multidisciplinary teaching technique

The first descriptor is a straight-up picture of the archive project that presents a teaching technique and applies that technique in its entirety to history. The second descriptor emphasizes a use of the archive—teaching. The third underscores the pedagogical dimension of the project. The fourth underlines the community benefit, and the fifth highlights the potential of this teaching technique to engage students in many arenas of study at the same time. All the descriptors overlap; none is exactly the same as any other.

Before we turn to the use that we will make of these descriptors to search grant databases, let us describe two additional projects in five different ways and see what else we might learn from the exercise. We have chosen two projects that are related in different ways to the archival project: One is the project on library preservation (Idea Sketch 2); the other is the pedagogical project involved with disseminating good teaching practice (Idea Sketch 3).

The library preservation project could be described as

- library preservation,
- large-scale book preservation,
- alternative preservation media,
- research libraries preservation strategy,
- organizational approaches to library preservation.

The project to disseminate exemplary teaching processes could be described variously as

- disseminating good teaching practices,
- networking teachers across classrooms and schools,
- adopting good teaching practices,
- rewarding innovation in teaching,
- private/public school cooperative teaching projects.

You can see that this exercise allows us to spread a wider net for identifying potential funding sources by taking advantage of the fact that a single project can have different starting points and different emphases. By looking across all three examples, we can notice that the exercise calls for both

- a brief description of the key elements of the project (starting point and major aspect), and
- an emphasis of a particular aspect of the project (teaching, organization, scale, preservation, library linkages, etc.).

With these project elements in hand, the stage is set to begin a database funding search, which is a highly efficient way to spread a wide net in a rather pointed fashion.

Searching Funding Databases

A funding database search is an intellectual exercise, not a mechanical process. Conducted well, it can provide us with an environmental scan of a field of inquiry. Our database search is part of a continuing review of literature and relevant electronic resources. To our knowledge of what is being published, it adds perspective on what is being supported and what is likely to be published in the future. In the best case, our search will yield comprehensive information on the funding terrain, which will help us develop our interests more thoughtfully and in a more market-sensitive fashion.

The details of database searches are easily learned and mastered. There is a fairly common electronic format for searching a funding profile. As we outlined above, the funding profile needs to be elaborated in associated but separable ways so that the search program can find the universe of outcomes we are trying to probe. Thus if we were interested in continuing education, we might enter into the profile "adult continuing education" and "lifelong learning" alongside "adult learning," "continuing education," and "Web-based learning." Given the imperfection of search engines, we are literally surrounding a topic with descriptors that will enable the electronic program to more fully explore our area of interest.

The specifics of search engines and the use of descriptors to find funding possibilities are not overly complex. Whether the database program is COS (Community of Science), IRIS (Illinois Research Information Science), RR (ResearchResearch), SPIN (Sponsored Program Information Network), or the search services and databases of the Foundation Center, the mechanics of the process are straightforward (see "Searching for Funding" inset). What is complicated is how to manage the output—or "hits"—and how to avoid getting caught up in storage and retrieval issues. Likewise, it is difficult to manage this output electronically; indeed, one faculty member we know developed a complementary nonelectronic filing system (essentially using a three-ring binder) that worked quite well for her and may work well for you.

Searching for Funding

The actual search for funding opportunities—the effort to link an idea that needs funding with a prospective source of financial support—is best viewed as a productive learning experience that sharpens the focus of scholarly inquiry.

The search for funding allows the researchers to scan the world of ideas that define the domain of proposed and funded research and locate their thinking in this larger realm of scholarly ideas. Indeed, the yield from a funding search can actually expand the vision and nuance of one's ideas. With this in mind, these funding tools are electronically based, easy to use, and generally available (free) through a college or university's Office for Sponsored Programs, which makes available to its research and scholarly communities one or more of the following funding opportunities databases (in alphabetical order):

COS (formerly Community of Science)—http://www.cos.com/

The Grant Advisor *Plus*—http://www.grantadvisor.com/

Grants.Gov (via the U.S. Government)—http://www.grants.gov

IRIS (Illinois Researcher Information Service)—http://gateway.library.uiuc.edu/iris/

ResearchResearch—http://www.researchresearch.com/

SPIN (Sponsored Projects Information Network)—http://www.infoed.org/

Another valuable tool for individuals outside of higher education is the Foundation Center, which provides a variety of tools to search grants databases as well as other information on foundations:

The Foundation Center—http://fdncenter.org

The faculty member was worried about losing electronically produced hits in e-mail files or in folders that grow inordinately large because of the ease of keeping them on hand electronically. She had a graduate student print out the funding opportunities and place them in a tabbed three-ring binder. The faculty member and the graduate student spent an hour or so every week reviewing the funding opportunities and matching them with the ongoing development of their research ideas and their continuing review of the literature. They kept the promising possibilities and jettisoned the others.

Besides producing more wieldy and useful files, the process built rapport around the collegial exploration of funding possibilities and the systematic development of research interest. The ongoing electronic/manual search became the basis for a successful working relationship that resulted in grant funding and an impressive number of coauthored books and articles.

The fundamentals underlying the process just described deserve an additional word or two. Specifically, a successful database funding search allows colleagues to nurture and grow ideas through ongoing reflection on the funding context. Managing the output of electronic searches manually and through dialogue allows a progressively more precise process to develop over time because colleagues are able to explore the inside, outside, and outskirts of an idea, probe it in different ways, and actually enjoy the soft ambiguity of the idea development process. The structuring of an idea—whether it is the idea of tectonic plates (a notion once laughed at and ridiculed) or the search for the generation of emotion (at once ineffable yet ever present)—yields in time to definition, the introduction of useful distinctions, and ultimately to rigorous analysis. The electronic search for funding is properly understood as an intellectual exercise aimed at further developing an idea by systematically searching and reviewing its context. As such, it is an exercise of sublime intellectual beauty and immense practical value.

Making Use of Initial Database Search Results

We may get really lucky and find in our initial database search a description of a previously funded project that sets the stage for, or complements in essential ways, the project we would like to propose. More likely, we will emerge from our database search with a number of potential funders or a number of RFPs (requests for proposals) that encircle our idea but do not touch down precisely where we would like to go. We are likely to encounter a rough, or approximate, match between our interests and those of a funder. Now we need to create a firm connection between our abiding interests and those of the funder that we perceive from our database search. In a word, we now need to do some additional research of our initial findings or hits in order to make the case for including our proposed idea under a funder's established guidelines.

With a potential funding source at hand, we want to prepare carefully for a real-time discussion of mutual interests. This we do by obtaining

- a detailed program of description of the funder's mission, vision, and programs (usually available readily via the Web),
- the name of a program officer working in the area encompassing our interest or idea (often provided in the RFP).

What may have been an initial list of 7 to 10 possible funding sources winnows down as additional detail begins to suggest that what appeared to be a possible match on the face of things in our broad-net search is not a match in fact. The detailed program description will be key in helping us better understand how good or complete the match is between our interests and those of the funder.

For those leads that still seem promising, we need to develop a letter of inquiry addressed to a specific program officer. The letter of inquiry employs our sketches and lays out in two pages or so what we have in mind, what we intend to accomplish, the outcomes we hope to produce, and the timeline and budget we require for the proposed project.

This introductory letter is our calling card. It introduces our interests in a thoughtfully formulated way. Perhaps the best way to demonstrate its utility is to provide an example. You will recognize the content from Idea Sketch 3 (idea originators and idea subscribers). Without saying much more, even our letters of inquiry build easily from the several related sketches of our idea (see Figure 3.1).

Figure 3.1   Sample Letter of Inquiry

Ms. Dana Pritchard
Vice President for Programs
Innova Foundation
East Mildred, IA 01101

Dear Ms. Pritchard:

Based on the Innova Foundation's interest in K–12 education and your emphasis on the need for innovative practices that make a difference in the lives of students and teachers, I would like to present an idea for a K–12 project that builds on the innovations that constantly take place in schools across the nation. I will briefly describe the core idea we have in mind, what we hope to accomplish, the outcomes we seek to produce, and the time and resources required to carry out the proposed project.

A number of colleagues have found that in almost every school, and certainly in every school district, there are teachers who constantly innovate. One will dream up teaching geometry through the construction of geodesic domes; another will find ways to teach language arts by establishing a school radio station; a third will teach art to special education students by having them silkscreen their designs on T-shirts.

We wondered aloud whether we might help teachers better engage in innovative teaching practices and thereby engage more fully with their students. We reasoned that teacher-developed innovations might travel from classroom to classroom, school to school, and district to district. The idea we hit upon was to fund practitioners to adopt and adapt these innovations and to honor the innovators for their insights and contributions to improved practice. We have come to believe that a systematic program of support for the two categories of teachers will improve the quality of instructional learning in classrooms and help students take up more active ways to pursue knowledge and skills.

To achieve the outcome of teachers more engaged in the educational lives of their students, we have in mind a number of tangible outputs. These include the following:

- A catalog of innovations in sufficient detail to allow for adoption/adaptation
- A series of small grants that will facilitate the work of the adopters/adapters
- A celebratory event that honors innovators, cites adopters/adapters, and provides public access to the inner working of this program

We estimate the cost of small grants to adopters/adapters to range from $100 to $300 each. The cost of the recognition ceremony we estimate at $2,000 to $3,000. Administration and the development of program materials (including catalogs) we place at $80,000 a year. Assuming a 2-year time frame, we can establish the administrative structure of an operating program in 2 to 3 months, disseminate program information by Month 6, decide on citations for innovators and awards for adopters/adapters by Month 11, and hold a celebratory event in Month 14. We would start a second round of applications for awards in Month 12 and make a second round of grants in Months 16 through 19. A second recognition ceremony would take place in Month 23.

Assuming 20 awards per wave, 2 awards ceremonies, and comprehensive administrative/materials services, the cost of the project would come to about $172,000 over the 2-year period.

We welcome your interest and your comments and especially an opportunity to talk with you in person.

Sincerely yours,

Mary Elaine Hartman

At the appropriate time, we follow up with a call to determine if our initial sense of interest is in fact realistic. The ensuing first conversation with the program officer is critically important in its own right. Indeed, before calling we need to reflect on possible discussion points. We need to be able to view our interests from the point of view of the funder and be prepared to engage the program officer in a discussion of the funder's interests, not just our own. In sum, we need to call with a purpose and a plan. During our call, the following is also important:

1. *We need to establish rapport.* That is, we need to establish trusting and thoughtful exchange as we engage in a give-and-take about what the funder seeks and how we might provide a means to the funder's programmatic ends.

2. *We need to take a collaborative approach.* That is, we need to take the position that we are helping the funder to realize the funder's high purposes by addressing a societal need through collaboration built on exchange.

In effect, we are saying to the funder: We have a fine-tuned piece of your program, one we believe fits with your overall mission and your programmatic vision. Taking this wider view of the funder's outlook helps place the exchange on a more even footing and also helps us see the exchange in perspective. That last point requires some detail.

A funder is in competition with other funders for scarce good ideas. By the power of logic, reason, and exchange, you need to convey that you have something precious to offer: a truly fine idea that can be implemented within the funder's guidelines for the benefit of many and to the credit of the sponsor.

Based upon an informal survey and numerous conversations we have had with program officers from federal agencies, state government, foundations, corporations, public charities, and professional societies, we consistently hear from program officers how they want to be engaged by ideas that produce a level of excitement and provide vision for a project or program. Stated negatively, the program officers consistently report to us that much of what they receive in written and oral form lacks vision, clarity, and appreciation of the funder's programmatic directions.

All told, a funder is looking for a good idea that fits with the funder's vision. Likewise, in attempting to understand the funder's point of view, it is best to do just that and *not* try to "edit the editor." We do not want to tell the program officer what she should want to fund or ought to fund. We want, instead, to fine-tune what we know we want to do—what we are committed to do—which is to align our ideas thoughtfully and well with the interests, guidelines, and constraints of the funder.

An Aside

The approach of this book is to begin with your ideas, not with a funder's interests. In your ideas reside personal and professional commitment, experience, and wisdom. You have spent precious time becoming a professional, and you have spent a career defining your interests, as well as your subject and methodological passions. You come with some ease to the formulation of ideas that have grown up inside you and blossomed in exchange with colleagues or in personal reflection. Our position is that the only way to develop authentic ideas that speak to you and serve others is to start with *your* notions, not those of funders.

To chase funding opportunities and twist oneself into contention for funding may produce momentary satisfaction if your proposed project is funded, but in the long run the positive result thus obtained may wind up with your feeling you have been sentenced to the hard labor of fulfilling the terms of a funded project whose objectives and ends are not truly your passion. Given that we are starting with your ideas and interests means that in all likelihood you will have to negotiate the final (marginal) differences between your proposal and the program guidelines of the funder. You will find that you can maintain your dignity, passion, and sense of purpose in that exchange without having to contort yourself or your ideas.

In the initial conversational exchange with the program officer, we are beginning to negotiate a shared mission: the ideas and interests we propose to pursue in common as a project or program. As we do so, we need to have in mind that part of the challenge for a program officer is *entering into your vision* because only by doing so can the officer make an intellectual contribution—not just a funding contribution—to your idea. For the program officer, this means offering suggestions that begin with your ideas and actively linking those ideas to the mission and vision of the funder (purposes and guidelines). It could also mean linking your proposed work to the work of others, offering suggestions for reworking elements of your proposed project, or connecting you with professionals at other institutions who are interested in aspects of what you are proposing.

We need to appreciate that program officers are expert in looking deeply into individual projects and broadly across programs. Indeed, they are expert at what may be termed *issue mapping*, or the laying out of issues and considering alternative ways of addressing them. We should seek both kinds of help and advice—deep understanding of what we are proposing and comparative analysis of our project vis-à-vis those of others—as we engage the program officer about our idea and the formulated project that flows from it. In the end, we are trying, alongside and in partnership with a program officer, to relate our idea to the funder's interests where the funder's issue mapping serves as the basis for programmatic approaches (mission and vision) and programmatic statements (guidelines).

Productive Exchanges With Program Officers

Let us venture a level or two deeper into the exchange with the program officer. Only on the basis of a viable exchange can we proceed with a formal proposal (see Chapter 4).

In the conversation itself, the program officer will be doing all of the following:

- Attending to the architecture your idea provides for the project
- Engaging you on aspects and details of the workability of your project idea and how you would implement it
- Actively relating the unfolding conversation to the issue mapping the funder has done and continues to pursue
- Vetting possible (nuanced) changes that could strengthen your project and further align it more closely with the funder's outlook and purposes

Based on this conversation, you will walk away with several possible messages. The starkest is that your idea does not conform to the funder's interests. Or you may instead hear a more gentle "no" from the program officer: "We are funding ideas that appear even more promising on the face of things than the idea you presented today." The most positive message you might receive requires a trained ear to hear: "There is a possible match between your idea and our funding interests."

Let's deal with the tough news first. If you have been discouraged from applying for funds, you need to reflect on what you have been told. Someone with experience in reviewing compelling proposals—in light of a particular outlook on funding opportunities (as they are called)—has determined the following:

- The idea is "out-of-program" (or "OOPs" as the inside lingo goes).
- The idea is "in program" but is not a priority.
- The idea is imperfect (not clearly described, not linked to the work of others, not compelling, etc.).

If the last message is received, we have something rather specific to learn from this outside review. We might best process it in consultation with our colleagues who helped give form and shape to the project idea. Together we can refashion what we have crafted, or we can decide what we have formulated deserves further consideration from other funding sources. Feedback, no matter the form it takes, can be enormously valuable to our work.

If you have not been discouraged from applying for funds, then and only then do you put together a customized proposal. The word *customized* is carefully chosen. We want to avoid what program officers often refer to as a *factory proposal* or *broadside* sent out in quantity in the hope that, if you send off enough of them, one will surely hit its target (an interested funder). This approach tarnishes individual and institutional reputations and has little to recommend it. Before you commit the time and energy to draft and redraft a thoughtful proposal, you want to have a sense that what you have worked hard to conceive and develop is of some interest to a funder.

While the "not discouraged from applying" message is hardly a resounding endorsement, do remember that the program officer needs to manage expectations and avoid premature commitments; nonetheless, you are now positioned to write a proposal that reflects your interests, and one that seems (initially at least) to match with those of the funder. You will learn to write the proposal by employing a few principles appropriate to an accomplished professional. The chapter on proposals follows.

Chapter Summary

By always emphasizing orderly and manageable progression, we have focused on engaging the funding literature as a way to begin taking account of the interests and approaches of others. We presented the process we follow including, most important, the initial step of describing the project idea in multiple ways. This step is key to entering a large and diverse database literature with search engines that employ so-called descriptors to make initial connections between your idea and the funding actions of sponsors. We continued the description of the process with how you might actually apply for funding. While it will always be helpful in developing a thesis or dissertation to survey the funding literature, it may be fully useful only in established professional careers to complete the steps presented in this chapter. That said, we think students and faculty should have the entire funding process in sight from the start.

REFLECTIVE QUESTIONS

In getting perspective on your idea from the vantage of the funding literature, we urge you to reflect on and ask questions about the nature of a funding point of view and how it differs from or complements your own viewpoint.

Range of Choices and Actions

1. Do you discern in the funding literature patterns for the types of projects funders have supported? Do you discern, or can you reasonably impute, reasons for these choices? How do these choices and rationales compare to yours?

2. What more refined choices can you discern in preference for scale, products, and timelines? Do you discern reasons for these choices? How do the choices and rationales compare to the reasoned choices you have made?

Strengths and Limitations of Funding Data

3. What are the strengths of funding databases, and when do you find yourself wanting to talk with a program officer?

4. Are there parallels in the academic sphere?

Organizing Programs

5. Do you perceive how funders might relate your idea to a larger program outlook?

6. Do you begin to see the outlines of a research program emerging from your core idea?

Contributions to Fields and Society

7. Do you discern a funding point of view toward the contribution of your type of project to a field of inquiry or to society?

8. How does your work help others with their inquiries or with their field of practice?

4

Proposals

Our purpose in this chapter is to demystify the writing of a proposal. To do that, we provide an overview of proposal sections followed by purposefully brief descriptions of what you should address in each. We also include an extended example so that you can follow a proposal development from start to finish. After describing each proposal section in this way, we comment on the overall proposal document from five vantage points. Our purpose is to provide you with a solid and constructive basis for understanding the nature and uses of the proposal in action.

With the proposal sections simplified and demystified, and the overall architecture of the proposal viewed from several perspectives, you are in a position to guide yourself through a writing process that helps clarify your thinking and present it in a lucid and compelling fashion.

Proposal Sections

A proposal is an intentionally repetitive art form that proceeds in sections from greater generality to greater specificity as it elaborates an idea as a project. In each of its sections, you cover the same idea, purposes, and activities in progressively greater detail as you proceed from higher to lower levels of abstraction in your discussion of the following:

- Core project idea
- Relationship to previous work or work of others
- Methods (their appropriateness, reliability, and validity)
- Activities
- Outputs/outcomes (potential relevance of findings and/or activities)
- Budget/budget justification and timeline

As we proceed from section to section, we revisit in greater detail what we propose to do, why, how, with what effect, at what cost, and in what period of time.

In proposal-like fashion, let us review the proposal categories we present above with more detail for each. We characterize the nature and purpose of each section and under each proposal heading provide a brief illustrative paragraph or two based on Idea Sketch 1, which described the teaching of history through archival holdings.

CORE IDEA: WHAT, WHY, WHO BENEFITS

In the opening section of the proposal—sometimes termed "Project Purpose" or "Description of the Project"—we present the core project idea. From the core idea, we segue easily and naturally into a broad and encompassing statement of why we should conduct the project, as well as who benefits. We state what we think this project will contribute to knowledge, scholarship, practice, social change, or some other high purpose, and we say who will benefit from its implementation.

For the archival teaching example we presented in Idea Sketch 1, the core idea is teaching history through a series of readings both forward and backward in time to arrive at a balanced historical interpretation. The proposed creative pedagogy is first and foremost a contribution to the practice of teaching history. Benefit will clearly accrue to students as they develop a fuller understanding of the value of source material along with a heightened ability to sift for veritas (truth). Institutional studies may also benefit: The study of history, language, economics, and social science can all be pursued simultaneously. Finally, local historical societies and local communities might well benefit from research employing community archives.

In all, a strong and compelling case can be made that an archival approach to the teaching of history is a pedagogical idea worth pursuing for its own sake, as well as for the sake of students, disciplines, and communities. In this section, as in all the others, you can state these points briefly or more fully, proposal page length permitting. You can also, with intellectual poise, explore the terrain of your idea in the proposal. You can evidence a move toward mastery of a subject that does not have altogether discrete boundaries. Most important though, you need to demonstrate that you have not lost yourself or your colleagues in the radii of your idea. Rather, with self-confidence, humility, and curiosity, you have walked around the periphery of your core idea and have found your way home to a point of confluence between your interests and those of a funder.

RELATIONSHIP TO THE WORK OF OTHERS: PROVIDING CONTEXT

You might find this proposal section labeled "Review of the Literature" or "Project Context." Still working with a fairly broad brush, we want to put our core idea in a context of related ideas and related projects. In so doing, we can address several key questions about the nature of our point of departure. Two questions guide our thinking:

- Are we extending the work of others, taking a new tack, rechecking findings, reaching toward a new synthesis, operating at a different scale, or working with different populations?
- What stands out most in the comparison of our proposed project to previous or ongoing work that is related on the face of things?

To demonstrate how our proposed work stands at a point of confluence with the work of others, we want to locate our project in a tradition of scholarship or practice. To do this, we need to describe how things have evolved historically and/or how things have been practiced in the past. Our manner is poised, but exploratory, as we prepare ourselves to nurture our idea through guided discovery.

What makes the archival project work unique is the exclusive use of source materials to teach history, the iterative/comparative method of sifting for stable findings, and the truly in-depth treatment of subject and topics. What links the proposed work to the field of pedagogy is (a) the underlying tension between teaching techniques that are generally useful versus those that appear unique to a particular discipline (here it is history), (b) the long-term conversation in the literature about survey approaches versus in-depth approaches to the teaching of content, and (c) the matter of developing teaching techniques that can be widely adopted and adapted, thus making them available and accessible to large numbers of practicing teachers. We would cite work in each of these arenas, show how our work is related, and describe how our work builds on the work of others *and* represents a rather new and promising point of departure.

METHODS: HOW WE WILL KNOW

We are getting more specific as we address how we are going to implement our core idea. Knowing that the section that follows this one focuses on specific project activities, we want to characterize our selection of activities here by describing our approach to implementation in terms of the methods we will employ in our project.

In the archival project, we follow two methodological paths. One pertains to teaching methods; the other to research methods. Under teaching methods, we will describe how we organize the class, the sequence of pedagogical activities and exercises, the nature of student and teacher responsibilities in the classroom, and so on. The idea is to give the funder, and eventually the professional teachers, a clear view of how we intend to organize project activities so they reflect an underlying teaching methodology.

Under research methods, we may want to list topical questions on which we will collect data or information. To be more specific, we want to learn the following from our pedagogical methods in action:

- How many students can usefully take an archive-based course at any one time?
- What opportunities exist for individual and joint student archival research, and what are the costs and benefits of each?
- Which inquiry topics lend themselves to the archival approach, and which do not?
- How much time is required (average and range) to reach stable historical findings for different types of inquiry topics?

The methods section for this particular project becomes a series of questions we ask to determine how we might improve the proposed course in the future. Methods for research projects, demonstration projects, or service projects may well address different sets of questions, but nevertheless share a dedication to learn from our proposed project how to accomplish our purposes more fully over time.

In the proposal, as well in the subsequent project reports, we need to demonstrate why our approach to scholarship is useful. Simply put, those concepts and tools we studied as graduate students—ranging from quantitative, qualitative, and mixed methodologies to methods for assuring validity and reliability (such as credibility, transferability, dependability, and confirmability)— are important components of scholarship, disciplined inquiry, and scholarly methodology. The combination of these integrated components helps us know what we have learned through our work and from our project.

ACTIVITIES: WHAT WE WILL DO

When we reach this section, we are revisiting the core idea as a series of action choices we have made, each valuable and justifiable in itself, with each linked in useful ways to the proposal sections that come immediately before and after. In short, in the activities section we are stating in rather discrete and finite terms just what we propose to do.

We can choose to follow this section with a timeline that represents activity headlines on a time-ordered graphic. Alternatively, we can include the timeline in the budget section where an altogether numerically detailed presentation awaits.

For the proposed archival project, the following list of course activities is instructive:

- Presentation of and training in basic archival research techniques
- Handling of archival materials and archival protocols

- Development of archival research assignments and their variations as individual or group projects
- Uses of classroom discussion
- Involvement of community members in classroom discussions

Within the guidelines provided by the funder on page length and pagination, you can go on about activities in detail. In the end, you must follow your own sense of providing enough detail so the reader fully understands how well prepared you are to carry out the proposed project.

OUTPUTS AND OUTCOMES: ACTIONS, DELIVERABLES, AND THEIR BENEFITS

We are poised to rehearse project outputs and outcomes with a statement of benefits attached to each. Plainly stated, it is not sufficient to list hoped-for results. While the outputs you enumerate must be realistically achievable, they must also be persuasive. Indeed, they must be linked to outcomes of meaningful purposes. Because outputs are specific in nature and tied to a timeline, a compelling description of project outcomes and their linkages to project outputs can help strengthen the case for project funding.

In enumerating outputs and outcomes, we are also addressing the ways in which we can evaluate the proposed project. We can do this in a separate proposal section titled "Evaluation," or we can link the discussion more directly and organically to project outputs (and the activities they depend on) and project outcomes (and the project outputs they rest on). We prefer the latter. Evaluation should serve to assess and improve. To achieve the latter requires keen attention to the project's stated purposes distinguished by what we will do (activities), what we will produce instrumentally and immediately (outputs), and what we ultimately accomplish (outcomes). We therefore would tend to embed evaluation in the section on project "Outputs and Outcomes."

All said, a project wends its way toward its goals. The rather straight line presumed among proposed activities, expected outputs, and anticipated outcomes inevitably encounter bends and twists. The proposal process itself begs the scholar to worry about deliverables and put aside the sidebars of thought, which emerge as part of the continuing development of the idea in the project's implementation. As we all grow more aware of the benefit of stating anticipated and unanticipated learning—as we grow more aware of the benefit of stating both negative and positive findings—we can usefully state in our proposal that we look forward to identifying additional outcomes that move an arena forward, no matter how we encountered them in the course of the proposed project.

For the archive project, we want to state explicitly what we will eventuate for students, teachers, the archive, the discipline of history and other areas of disciplinary study, and the community. Specific benefits that might well accrue include the following examples:

- Creative student research reports that raise the level of undergraduate study
- Presentations on campus, at community venues, and at history association meetings on archive-based teaching methods and specific research findings
- Demonstrated increases in foreign language project or proficiencies in other fields of academic study (political science, rhetoric, law, etc.), as facilitated by the nature of the archive in use
- Demonstrated uses of findings for historical societies
- Demonstrated uses for local communities

Along with these specific outcomes, you might provide a sense of timing, priority, and interconnection of results. As you do so, you begin to feel the proposed project taking on the qualities of an initiative in formation. Things are becoming real.

BUDGET: AT WHAT COST OVER WHAT PERIOD OF TIME

In this section, we recognize that the timeline and the budget are really two aspects of the same presentation. As we go over the elements of the budget, we recognize the presence of an underlying timeline. In the budget proper, we make time an explicit variable as we consider the following factors:

- People × Time
- Equipment × Time
- Activities × Time
- Special project needs × Time
- Other × Time

A matrix of projects needs (down the left side) and project timing (across the top) provides the framework for a persuasive budget—one that says we will manage funds with uses and timing always in mind.

As we fill in the budget matrix, we employ the budget categories as a checklist for careful review and scrutiny of the project narrative. Whatever appears in earlier project sections with a cost attached to it must appear in the budget. Mostly we will focus on the "Activities" section. However, we will want to review the entire proposal from a budgetary point of view just in case we incurred an expense item along the way not fully reflected as a project activity.

Figure 4.1   Sample 3-Year Budget Planner

Budget Categories	Year 1	Year 2	Year 3
I. Personnel	$	$	$
• Salary and wages			
• Fringe benefits			
• Consultant and contract services			
• Evaluation consultant			
II. Nonpersonnel	$	$	$
• Space costs			
• Rental, lease, purchase of equipment			
• Supplies			
• Travel			
III. Other costs	$	$	$
• Insurance (fire, theft, liability)			
• Conference tuition, etc.			
• Telephone			
• Postage			
IV. Indirect costs	$	$	$
Total project cost	$	$	$

The relationship of the budget to the timeline is critically important. They come together as a joint discipline that guides our final activity choices and helps us understand how much Y or Z dollars can accomplish or purchase over a specified period of time. In addition, the budget guides scale by asking how much can we accomplish in what period of time given Y or Z dollars? In a sense, dollar resources are always scarce, as are resources associated with professional talent, effective administrative management, and institutional support. The budget helps you understand what you can accomplish, in what period of time, with what dollars, with what human resources, and with various levels of organizational support.

An Aside

You might try the exercise of increasing your target budget by 50% and decreasing it by the same proportion to see what you would add and what you would cut. This important exercise effectively demonstrates how proposed projects are always relative to available resources, that project scope and timing can be altered (within limits) to accommodate budgetary increases and decreases, and that making seemingly absolute statements about resources—for example, the funder's allowable budgets are not adequate to conduct the project—are not always accurate. Simply stated, given what we propose, we either need more resources, or we need to cut the proposed scope, scale, and outcomes to align resources with effort.

For the archives project, the budget is straightforward:

- Salary for the director (release time to develop the course and work on contacts inside and outside the institution involving the uses of archival studies for community benefit)
- Supplies (usual and specialized supplies, including access to large-format copying equipment and required supplies)
- Travel (to conferences and meetings)
- Dissemination (how you plan to share findings, experience, and knowledge)
- Evaluation (of what was done and its overall impact)

The timeline would present work on the course syllabus early in the project, contact with professional academics and end users throughout the project, dissemination activities as findings become available, and summative evaluation when the project is completed.

At the end of the budget request we submit to the funder, we also present the budget we are offering as institutional support. If the idea we are presenting and its manifestation as a project are worthy of external support, then surely they are worthy of (realistic) internal support as well.

In the pedagogical project we have used as an example throughout this chapter, the major contributed institutional expenses are additional personnel and infrastructure costs to maintain extended student access to the archive. This dollar figure, alongside all of the figures for major categories of the budget, should be explained in a budget narrative (sometimes called a *budget justification*). This is another opportunity to persuade the funder that each and every proposed expenditure brings value and meaning to the project. In as much detail as you wish to muster, you can explain the inner workings of a project that is becoming more palpable and real with each sentence.

In sum, a good idea needs to be fiscally responsible, not fiscally creative. The idea needs to project fiscal responsibility; thus we thus think it a good idea to craft the budget with the advice of a fiscal adviser. You will receive guidance that translates into direction. Importantly, you should not edit the budget editor, nor should you attempt to make the budget creative. The budget is the equivalent of "black letter law." It is what the project says. In detail and in derivation, the project narrative drives the budget outline and specifics. What the narrative says, the budget must reflect faithfully, honestly, and openly.

Chapter Summary

Everything comes together in the statement of the proposal. Your initial sketches of your idea and its attendant costs, outputs/outcomes, scale, and timeline are still discernible. They may be deepened by the interests and outlooks you encountered in the funding literature. The proposal statement extends your earlier work systematically as it presents what you will address—in a full statement of your core idea—along with how you will proceed, what you will produce, when, and at what cost. Importantly, the proposal allows you to place your idea and the project that flows from it in an intellectual context so that your work can indeed contribute to knowledge and/or practice.

The proposal guide we offered emphasized a semistandard set of proposal categories. These categories will be useful to you as a student and as a professional because they offer a progression that will never go out of style. To recap briefly, in the proposal you begin with a broad statement of your core idea. Section by section, you state—or restate—how your idea relates to the work of others, what methods you will employ to explore your idea, and what outcomes your idea will produce over what period of time and at what costs. Your idea in its depth and breadth will guide all sections of the proposals. Understanding the role of that thread and the somewhat repetitive form that follows its function will enable you to turn your sketches into a rigorous and precise project proposal.

REFLECTIVE QUESTIONS

As you reflect on your proposal, we would urge you to consider the following categories and the major questions in each:

Alignment

1. Does the proposal align your interests with those of the funding literature and most assuredly with those of the academic literature?

In an honest way, and not in a contrived or superficial manner, the proposal should rightfully claim to further the programmatic interests of funders and further deepen academic knowledge.

2. Does the proposal align across its several sections?

What holds the proposal together is its core idea. Each section, as it adds detail and substance, must do so in alignment, or consonance, with everything that comes before and all that comes after. For example, if we say that part of our core idea is to link our archival project to the social needs of the community, then each section that further specifies the nature of the work proposed must refer in one fashion or another to community outreach.

3. Have you literally reviewed the proposal to assess alignment?

The best way we have found to ensure alignment across proposal sections is to read the proposal by section going forward and then backward. Going forward, once a theme is struck or once a detail is added, we want to check subsequent sections for consistency. Starting at the end with the budget, we can put together a checklist of proposal elements. As we move backward through the proposal sections, those elements should be in plain view, especially in the section on project activities. As we move further forward toward the front end of the proposal, there should be no surprises. All themes and elements should already appear on the checklist.

Persuasiveness

4. Is each section of the proposal compelling? More specifically, are the early sections of the proposal persuasive calls to action? Are the latter sections compelling descriptions of a project we can envision in action?

Persuasiveness is not a negative. If truly compelling, an academic colleague, not unlike a funder, will respond with "aha!"s to a proposal that clarifies, extends, or deepens a request for proposal or further refines a scientific viewpoint. In fact, in both cases, the highest compliment is that the proposal respects the past and ventures boldly into the future.

A compelling statement is, among other things, an expression of enthusiasm. When honestly arrived at, it has an infectious quality, one that gathers up the energy of others even as it expresses commitment to a proposed project that matters. Your personal enthusiasm, which should be evident in every section of the proposal, lets funders and advisers know that you care about the work you propose and will take pains to produce ends that you are professionally and personally committed to.

Planning

5. Does the proposal present in ordered stages carefully laid plans for conducting the project's work?

A wit has said that even Moses could not get his people across the Red Sea (or the Sea of Reeds, according to recent scholarship) without a plan that managed information, reduced stress, and resulted in compelling action. Moses managed his planning with divine help. How to manage project planning is not something we necessarily learn in graduate school with divine guidance or with the help of professors; rather, it is something that we need to reflect on. The proposal statement affords that opportunity.

6. Does the proposal have in it a project management plan, or a schema for getting the work done in a concentrated, delineated period of time with adequate staff and supplies and with a strong guiding idea?

The section on project activities will benefit from a project management perspective, and the budget, while making sense in and of itself—things must indeed add up—can also provide discipline regarding how we will allocate our resources, no matter how scarce they may appear.

Wending and Winding

7. Are you prepared for the very real possibility that while the proposal will serve as a launch point and provide ongoing directional guidance, the research project will wend and wind its way to its conclusion?

The proposal is our very best guess of useful starting points for concerted programmatic action. It is also a best guess of what we will actually do, in what order, and at what cost in time and effort. Indubitably, our plans will shift as we hit the ground. A thoughtful researcher, not unlike a thoughtful funder or colleague, understands and expects this. For all, the proposal is a guiding document, one that lays out useful connections. It is a helpful reference as we wend our way from agreed-on starting points to agreed-on deliverables.

5

Managing a Funded Project

Managing a Project

The personal characteristics and professional skills that enable someone to develop an original idea, systematically identify appropriate sources of funding, and write a successful proposal may not be the same attributes that enable one to implement, manage, and bring to a useful conclusion a thesis, dissertation, or an extramurally funded project.

Take heart. No matter your level of experience in managing projects, programs, or groups of people, you can build on the work that went into developing the proposal while treating explicitly and candidly the additional requirements for conducting and concluding a project.

In this chapter and at the end of this book, we want to make the educational point that all research projects—funded and unfunded—benefit from a management perspective. In the case of graduate student research, learning how to manage a dissertation project is a dress rehearsal for managing a funded project. And while we will devote the substance of this chapter to managing funded projects, we will take the liberty of posing parallels between managing both types of projects and about the ways in which managing a dissertation project is similar to managing a funded project and the ways in which it is not. You may be surprised to find that the two are more alike than they are dissimilar.

We organize our discussion of managing a funded project around three basic principles:

1. The proposal you developed and submitted to the funder is the key tool for implementing your sponsored project.

2. As principal investigator (PI) or project director (PD), you are a CEO with all the rights and responsibilities pertaining thereto.

3. The project you lead will produce outcomes in more directions than you originally proposed.

49

First principle: The proposal you developed and submitted to the funder is the key tool for implementing your sponsored project.

The proposal can help you get started and serve as a touchstone as the project encounters unanticipated twists and turns. The proposal can also act as a thoughtfully developed checklist of expected outcomes that can help guide a funded effort.

While the project proposal is both a starting point and an enduring touchstone, it is not and cannot be a complete guide to the conduct of a funded project. You, like others before you, will find that the project will wend its way. Promising avenues of advance may close down, and more promising ones open as you implement the project and gain experience.

Second principle: As PI or PD, you are a CEO with all the rights and responsibilities. You will be called upon to exercise leadership in a variety of ways:

- Hiring staff
- Developing a micro-organization
- Assigning specific project tasks based on a reasoned division of effort
- Monitoring project progress
- Making necessary midcourse corrections
- Maintaining a productive liaison with funders
- Safeguarding the rigor and purposes of the project
- Acting as the public face of the initiative
- Writing and submitting progress reports
- Being accountable for all project expenditures and financial commitments
- Developing strategies for disseminating findings to a variety of audiences
- Becoming a resource for others who are interested in your topic, your research, and your findings

We will take up each of your duties in turn as we describe a position filled with promise and excitement that need not be overwhelming in its entirety.

Third principle: The project you lead will produce outcomes in more directions that you originally proposed.

You will learn much by serving as the head of a funded project. While not exactly a bully pulpit, a funded project is a stable platform from which you gain firsthand knowledge of what in a delimited field of interest seems to work, what does not, and where you and others might usefully head in the future. By the conclusion of a successfully conducted project, you will have earned the right to serve the public good by describing with detail what you learned, and where you think colleagues, informed citizens, and policy makers might usefully promote work in the future. With this in mind, let us take up these organizing principles in the order in which we presented them.

The Proposal and the Project

Between submitting the proposal and receiving funding, some of the most precious resource of all has passed by: time. The proposal, written in the recent past, has passed into historical time. When it was written, it was the very best, most accurate, most up-to-date statement we could produce. In fact, it may well have been a contribution to knowledge. Now funded, it may be dated. At the very least, several of its sections deserve a second visit.

In that simple, but chilling word *dated* lies the first task of the project: Update the proposal quickly and sensibly so that it can better guide initial forward progress. The easiest way to do this is to review each of the sections of the proposal and determine, with the help of colleagues working on the project, what investments of time and effort in revising the proposal will pay dividends in project start-up and longer-term management.

Let us go back over the key sections of Chapter 4 to gain a sense of where, and under what circumstances, updates are warranted.

CORE IDEA: WHAT, WHY, WHO BENEFITS

It is highly probable that the *what* and *why* of our core idea have not changed much, if at all. What might have changed some is *who benefits*. With time, we may have seen or actually experienced the interests of additional professional and public audiences in the nub of our proposal. For purposes of early networking—and certainly for purposes of later dissemination—we should consider paying additional attention to a new or nascent constituency interested in the core idea of our funded project.

We can update things easily by meeting with the project team and asking for input and advice. Only a few calls need be made and a few e-mails sent to check our perceptions with those of colleagues near and far. We can make good use of the efficiency and power of modern communications to check on rather recent developments. If colleagues are nearby, face-to-face meetings are particularly valuable for exchanging ideas, establishing high methodological standards, and beginning the hard work of maintaining quality communications among the project staff.

RELATIONSHIP TO THE WORK
OF OTHERS: PROVIDING CONTEXT

Here is where we would do well to spend some time and effort updating our working knowledge of related research in progress or formally reported in publications.

Sometimes things change fairly rapidly, even in the world of research, and we want to be certain to check the recent literature for major studies of possible interest, especially those in cognate fields. We may also want to consult with colleagues for their thinking on new projects, new data, and new publications, even if we are lifelong students of the area. In many arenas, professionals train for long periods and practice their crafts over long-lived professional careers. This was certainly the case for the archive/pedagogy project we described in Chapter 4. Even for that project we would want to take pains to ensure that our account of related work in both fields is altogether current. Electronic media might change the way we access some archives; in turn, the nature of access might affect or change our pedagogical approach to learning history from archival documents.

We will want to update our literature reviews regularly and frequently over the course of the project to ensure currency. Looking ahead to the second part of this chapter—where we take up project management—updating the literature review is an assignment the PI will want to make early on in the start-up phase. It is advisable to require that written updates be made available to the entire project team at least every 3 months or on a timetable agreed on by the research team. Even if one is working independently and with little or no input from colleagues, such updates are invaluable and truly a mark of mature scholarship.

METHODS: HOW WILL WE KNOW?

For purposes of the discussion thus far, we have assumed that the budget we requested for the project is the budget we were awarded. If this is the case, then we will likely want to begin the project with the methodology as we proposed it. Methods are key to a successful project. In the development of the proposal and in the conduct of its review, methodological rigor and appropriateness figured prominently. Indeed, the only circumstance in which we might want to consider updating or revising the methodology is when facing real and substantial budgetary changes that impact the project directly. Put differently, we will want to gauge the magnitude of any change in the amount of the award to ensure, on the one hand that the project is doable, and on the other hand that the essence of the project has not been compromised.

Financial change of whatever magnitude—from exigency to marginal cutbacks—affords, if not demands, a thorough check of the continuing viability of the methods proposed. For example, in the archival project we employed to develop the sections of a modal research proposal, there were two methodological prongs. One pertained to teaching methods, the other to research methods. These two sets of methodologies intertwined. In the face of budget rescission, a sensible choice might be to investigate a smaller number of pedagogical methods and thereby cut back on the number and types of research methods we employ.

A word more about the magnitude of change a project might face, as we want to be clear that the project as submitted benefited from careful consideration and reconsideration of what was possible in a bounded period of time with a specified level of resources. Changes in resource level affect not only what we can do but when we can produce results. Resetting project resources after the fact must of necessity spark a round of realigning resources, timing, and methods with each other. In any case, regular and final project reports will likely begin with a recitation of the proposed scope of methods and trace the decisions and trade-offs that resulted in a resource-appropriate design.

ACTIVITIES: WHAT WE WILL DO

Unless lightning has struck in the interim, the activities section should remain largely unchanged. While reflection is usually good, the PI/PD must take care to avoid an array of blocks, such as writing blocks, management blocks, and blocks resulting from endless conversations or a permanent state of reflection. Your initial sense of how the project might work best will probably still serve well as a jumping-off point. Second and third thoughts are not necessarily better than first thoughts, especially if first hunches will soon gain feedback from the rigors of implementation.

If the budget has changed significantly, the activities sections must change in a crafted and detailed way. What the project will do, when, for how long, and with what staff and which resources all need to be "costed out," so to speak, and re-presented in revised Gantt charts. There really is little alternative, for to conduct and complete a new version of the originally proposed project (the theme of the third section of this chapter), you must actively realign staff and other resources with new budget realities. Figure 5.1 shows what a typical Gantt chart looks like.

Figure 5.1   Gantt Chart

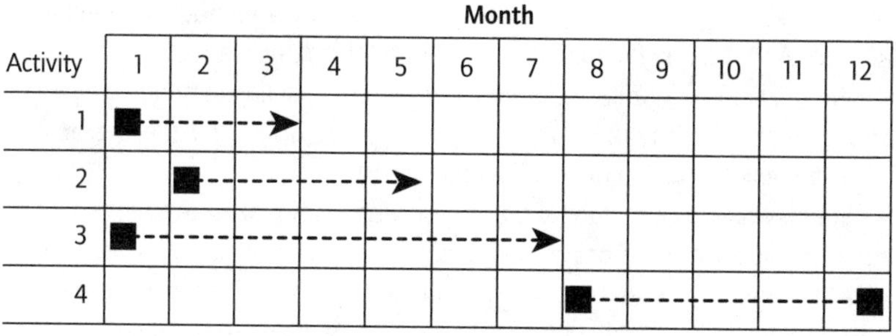

Here is the thinking behind the representation activity by time: Time waits for no one. Perennially a favorite phrase of parents and teachers alike, now you discover it is also a mantra for funded research projects. To manage this precious resource, you need to explain, or at least represent, how you intend to use time to the best advantage. A Gantt chart enables you to present activity by time and gives you and others an overview of what happens when.

Order and priority: In the simple representation in Figure 5.1, you see activities and the time order in which they take place along with their duration. Order added to duration yields priority. You can literally see the priority you are placing on topics and the resources you are allocating in the simple Gantt chart portrayal of project activities.

Intersections: Looking across activities by time, order, and duration, you are able to see the sum total of project effort taking place at any moment in project time. This is key to the allocation of very scarce human resources as measured in percentages of time, or "time-and-effort" to use the apt accounting and auditing term. The very useful and simple Gantt chart allows you to see how much is under way at any point in time, and thus gauge when high-demand times for project personnel will occur.

An Aside   Learning and Coping Strategies

Every funded project encounters challenges: Personnel leave, promising avenues of analysis close off, or unforeseen opportunities appear. In every case, it is our preference to engage challenges with a *learning strategy* and make every effort to avoid employing a *coping strategy*. For us, a learning strategy is a solution-based strategy, while a coping strategy is a way to temporize and buy time.

Where things are working well—where individuals with their personal learning styles have melded themselves into a high-performing group with its own learning style—we are able to make use of a number of learning strategies that apply broadly across a variety of challenges:

We may opt for a *formal learning strategy* that includes attending workshops, seminars, and other learning venues to pick up technical and practical experience of others on, say, compliance issues.

We may employ an *informal learning strategy* that makes excellent use of networks and conversations to deal with a specific issue, say, a decision to delay the collection of data pending another review of an insight or research-based nuance unattainable by a single team member working alone.

Likewise, we may find ourselves relying some on an *incidental learning strategy* that recognizes experience-based lessons as they occur.

We make use of *a collaborative learning strategy* where team members synthesize their individual and collective experience to produce an insight unattainable by a single team member working alone.

It seems to us that each of these learning strategies is superior and preferable to a coping strategy, which views challenges as sources of stress. Whether it is a deadline that needs to be met or a set of university rules that needs to be clarified, rather than employ a coping strategy to reduce uncertainty or minimize damage on the down side of things, we would prefer to avoid or get out of a coping strategy mode altogether. Our constant preference is for a learning strategy mode that promises good effects alongside recognition of lessons that can be played out again in the future.

OUTCOMES: DELIVERABLES AND THEIR BENEFITS

Revisiting outcomes enables us to apply reflection born of time to the litany of useful outcomes we originally promised. Even if the project remains largely as planned, the passage of time affords the opportunity to think harder and in greater depth about what we can produce that is of value to others.

The mantra we employed above applies here: If the budget has changed, it is very likely that the deliverables will change as well. Before the project gets under way is the best time to realign outcomes with newly defined constraints. The exercise is likely to be positive and reassuring. Creativity got us to the point where we turned an idea into a funded project. Creativity can take us to a redefined project that makes the best and most efficient use of available resources.

BUDGET/TIMELINE: WHAT RESOURCES FOR HOW LONG

We have learned to turn to our budget for a disciplined approach to the allocation of effort and resources. In the planning mode, we looked to the budget to give us a sense of what was possible, over what period of time, and with what level of resources. In a replanning mode, we can take two distinctively different approaches to our budget, depending on budgetary circumstances.

If the budgeted amount has not changed, we can take a long look at how we decided to deploy resources and ask if this is still our best sense of how to match funds and opportunities. It is too early in the project to start changing the budget in any significant way. It is not too early, however, to read the budget as a document having its own story to tell of how this project plans to link extramural funding to the initiative's purpose. You will find, we believe, that the budget does have a story to tell; one which provides insight above and beyond the figures that went into building its several parts.

If the budgeted amount has changed, then we should employ budgetary discipline to determine how best to allocate resources up and against a changed scale of effort. If we follow the prescriptions presented above, we have systematically considered each section of the proposal affected by budgetary change. Now is the opportunity to summarize our revisions as budgetary decisions that line up with each other in a numerical document that overviews resources and time. Having gone through the project budget exercise honestly and earnestly the first time around, we are fully prepared to recast the budget as a useful guide for our project efforts.

QUICK SUMMARY

Rereading the project proposal is an invitation to look back with pleasure on the clarity we have achieved and look forward with assurance to our replanning as we prepare to launch a funded effort designed to make a concerted contribution to knowledge, practice, and/or society. Having taken proposal development seriously—and having enjoyed its call to clarity and cooperation—we are well positioned to rethink with confidence and thoughtfulness what we have written and what we need to write again. This is an important step in the final preparation for launching the proposal. The next step is to step into the CEO role and roll things out.

Why Include Project Management?

Why, in a book that addresses research as varied as a doctoral dissertation and funded research involving postdoctoral students and faculty, include a chapter on project management? For one thing, all research projects need to be managed. For another, as doctoral candidates and postdoctoral students take on larger and more complex research projects, they will need to manage not only themselves and the resources available to them but others and the resources—including extramural funding—available to the group. Moreover, in a successful model of professional academic development, doctoral and postdoctoral projects should be guided in the knowledge that funded research projects are virtually always headed by PIs and PDs who hold doctorates.

In very practical terms, there is concern in academic circles for what is called *time-to-completion* for doctoral degree candidates. Every 10 years or so, the National Research Council (NRC) surveys academic departments at selected schools to discern the relationship between the country's investment in higher education and how many students complete advanced degree study and the time they take to do so. Time and other considerations—nature of degree support, including presence or absence of advising and mentoring—cannot begin to depict or make sense of the joy or agony students might experience as they make the shift from consumers to producers of intellectual work. It also cannot capture how much they would have benefited from learning how to manage their doctoral research studies as part of their graduate work.

Preproposal doctoral seminars are taking hold as departments, and sometimes universities as a whole commit themselves to provide support and guidance to dissertation candidates. Postproposal seminars are also growing in numbers as faculty and administrators more fully comprehend and appreciate NRC-type findings as a call for a completion strategy for graduate student degree candidates. We believe that such a strategy must perforce recognize that the formulation of ideas cannot stand apart from helping to ensure the successful completion of the dissertation. While pre- and postproposal guidance are essential, that guidance must include the hitherto untaught realm of project management.

The professional conduct of a funded project is what we turn to next. We end with the applicability of project management practices for doctoral-level research initiatives. As we address the first topic, you will find that you will link the several management dimensions in line with your own management style. Rather than attempt to divine in prospect how you will manage, or what management style you may find yourself employing, we suggest that you familiarize yourself with the rudiments and make use of them in a style and manner that fits you well.

The PI/PD as CEO

What does it mean for a PI or PD to take on the role of CEO? In the broadest of terms, it means thoroughly acquainting oneself with the rigors of project management. It also means learning new skills, especially those of working with and through others on both the administrative and content sides of the project.

To get started, we will take up some general points of guidance. We will then turn to the list of rights and responsibilities, or R&Rs, we presented earlier and visit each in turn. We believe that the more general orienting points and the more specific R&Rs are helpful in carrying out the complex but manageable role of being a CEO of a funded project.

POINTS OF ORIENTATION

By the time your project has received support, you have already taken on the largest and most demanding tasks of a project CEO: You have developed a vision sufficiently compelling to colleagues and funders to turn a project that merits funding into a project that has received funding. Now your tasks include turning an extramurally funded project in a meaningful initiative that meets or exceeds the expectations of colleagues, stakeholders, and funders.

In brief, you are now in the business of balancing the standards of management with the standards of research. To make the point bluntly, a lack of management standards puts the project under stress and puts objectives and standards at risk. High management standards thoughtfully acted on greatly increase the chance for successful outcomes.

A PI must employ a diverse set of skills (see specific R&Rs) while serving as a player/manager. Put differently, you cannot play every project position. If you developed the proposal alone, then now you will be asking people at your institution and people on the project staff to help manage it and do portions of its work. If you coauthored the project, then you may need to expand the team of co-investigators to include, as necessary, additional managerial expertise.

Before you take up any of the specific points that follow, you will find that good overall management begins with shared project management and trusted intraproject communication. In the review of the proposal at the first meeting of a management team, the group most often begins to appreciate project imperatives as shared responsibilities. With a purposeful focus mainly on themselves, they may want to consider changes in the availability, circumstances, level of interest, or level of commitment of project staff. Together they are also considering (a) what funding looks like; (b) what restrictions, if any, funders have placed on project activities; (c) what changes in scope funders may have put in place; (d) what subcontractual obligations may need attention; and (e) anything else that helps to give project staff a sense that the rigors of implementation are real yet finite and manageable.

At this moment in the formation of the project team, the PI/PD would do well to ensure the assembled group that there will most certainly be periods of confusion and stress. During those times, the research process benefits greatly from a commitment to sound project management that pays attention to the mechanics of getting a research-oriented operation—with several interacting parts—to move steadily toward its targeted aims of inquiry. All will soon learn that inquiry is not an unlimited process, but a bounded process that reaps rewards from being surrounded by a project team that allows the PI/PD to guide and facilitate refinding traction to keep everything moving forward.

In this open and honest initial conversation, you will come to appreciate almost immediately the unanticipated, and oftentimes extraordinary, talents team members bring to the project's tasks—indeed, talent, vision, and leadership that often go far beyond knowledge, commitment, and effort. What you might find daunting, colleagues might find interesting. Where you think the project will require more specialized talent, staff members may offer to go beyond defined duties because of interest and dedication.

In one project one of the authors was associated with, the problem of access to large educational systems was looming large from the start. As CEO, he had an evolving, but not developed, idea of how to open these systems to systematic research inquiry in the space of time allotted to the project. The associate project director came to the fore as an expert in cold calls, or telephone calls placed without benefit of prior introduction. With ease she placed telephone calls to public education administrators in several states, always to good effect. It is honest to say that she herself did not know she had such talents. Her interests led her to the tasks, and her talents took her and her project colleagues all the way home. During this stressful period, the PI maintained a viable organizational process that facilitated a most useful outcome.

While a second review of the proposal is under way during the first few weeks of the project, you can visit in a preliminary way with academic departmental administrators and central university administrators (e.g., deans and associate deans, directors of sponsored programs, and intellectual property offices, regulatory and compliance officers, departmental administrators, etc.) to let people know you are getting your project up and running and to also let them advise you on the range of management services and other research support they can provide. From managing time-and-effort reports to learning about potential conflicts of interest and producing timely project reports for funders, you will find that those who have come this way before will be eager to lend you a hand. In taking on the management of a funded project, you have joined a collectivity of researchers (or as one seasoned academic fondly refers to as a "gloat of research administrators") who are quite serious about conducting high-quality inquiry at a level extending one's reach through thoughtful and effective project management. You will be welcomed, mentored, and honored all at the same time.

As we turn to the more specific functions of the project CEO, it may be helpful to keep in mind that this position is a cornerstone for developing and adjusting the project vision, developing and redeveloping a project team, and sculpting a process for forward movement that makes good use of project and institutional infrastructure. It is a job with several identifiable and separable parts. Let us consider all of them in detail.

CHECKLIST OF PROJECT MANAGEMENT ITEMS

As indicated earlier, in the job description of the project CEO, all of the following leadership roles may apply:

- Hiring staff
- Developing a micro-organization

- Assigning specific project tasks based on a reasoned division of labor
- Monitoring project progress
- Making midcourse corrections
- Maintaining liaison with funders
- Safeguarding the rigor and purposes of the project
- Acting as the public face of the initiative
- Writing and submitting progress reports
- Being accountable for all project expenditures and commitments
- Developing strategies for disseminating findings to a variety of stakeholders and audiences
- Serving as a resource for others

As we work our way through the list, you will see how these duties intertwine in very interesting ways. We begin with the duties themselves and develop interlinkages as we make our way through the list.

HIRE STAFF

Hiring staff is both time-consuming and necessary. If you have done it before, you know how challenging it can be to assess qualities of mind and depth of experience that lead to position-based contributions to the project, all the while keeping open the possibility for lending help with tasks not yet specified but surely to be encountered as the project progresses forward.

Given the very special challenges of managing a project for which support and staff are scheduled from the start to terminate on a certain date, you are searching for a mix of adequacy on the experience/knowledge side of things along with high intelligence and curiosity in the more general scheme of things. The trade-offs can be stark. Where the position is technical, knowledge qualifications must be squarely met; where the position is more in the realm of support, knowledge and/or experience can sometimes be traded off in favor of generalist qualifications that allow for flexible use of personnel over the course of the project.

As creative and disciplined as you were when developing your project statement as a compelling proposal, so too must you be thoughtful and ingenious in linking project positions with talents serving stated goals that cannot be fully anticipated. The human resources (HR) department will understand these personnel needs and can be helpful in determining what you need to consider in reviewing applications and making offers. For example, the hiring of personnel on a funded project may differ markedly from standard HR practices for hiring staff solely funded by university resources. Knowledge of differences and nuances in university procedures can eliminate problems and help assure the cooperation of key university administrators who are anxious to see your project succeed.

DEVELOP MICRO-ORGANIZATIONS

No matter the project, if it involves three or more participants (PIs and co-PIs included), you must create an organizational structure. It may be a very flat structure with few intermediaries between or among project staff. Alternatively, if the project is large, complex, and one requiring a number of personnel, it is likely to be organized around functions whose members may change over time.

In a word, rehearsing several possible organizational alternatives takes us only so far. More valuable by far is for the project CEO (with co-PIs where appropriate) to consider organizational approaches for idea management, data management, information flow, methodological review, analysis and synthesis, and the dissemination of findings. Equally important is revisiting from time to time structural decisions taken initially.

Projects are not organizations that persist over large stretches of time. They are perhaps best viewed as micro-organizations embedded in a larger structure that need to maximize individual contributions from the start, as well as develop a capacity for making rapid adjustments as the project makes its way to and from promising avenues of activity.

ASSIGN SPECIFIC TASKS BASED
ON A REASONED DIVISION OF EFFORT

After the larger organizational alternatives have been considered, we need to get staff started on specific tasks based upon a division of effort that (a) plays to the strengths that each person brings and (b) ensures communication among all staff. To help make these points come alive, consider just how scarce the resources of time, money, and talent are in every funded project. You have carefully developed budgets that cover all three—time, money, and talent—and funders have reviewed your calculations and plans initially at their staff level and later again at their board level. The result may be justly characterized as an adequate, but never munificent, amount of money to support necessary talent for a delimited period of time. With all the care and consideration that have gone into planning the project budget, there is probably not a lot of wiggle room to change things fundamentally.

Operationalizing positional responsibilities as a set of initial start-up tasks is crucial to the efficient use of human and other resources. Revising the assignment of specific tasks in altogether timely ways—biweekly or even weekly—is a usual norm for sponsored project management.

MONITOR PROJECT PROGRESS

Monitoring project progress across specifically assigned tasks is an art in itself. We return once more to our example of choice: Because things tend to be interconnected—setting up pedagogical alternatives for using archives as tools for teaching students may require—in actual implementation—careful development of two or three teaching approaches, the recruitment of students, the development of measurement devices, and so on. Here we need to keep "critical path" items aligned with all the other considerations we are balancing. We may want to employ project Gantt charts that are much more specific than anything we presented for proposal review. We may also want to move staff around (the generalist point made earlier becomes very real at this juncture), as we seek to reallocate staff to keep the project progressing overall.

Rather than consider any of this an unfortunate turn of events, we should instead think of it as normal and expected. Embracing the management challenges of monitoring progress in an active way is the mark of a successful leader and a successful project in the making.

MAKE NECESSARY MIDCOURSE CORRECTIONS

Let us pause to consider the sum of positive outcomes for all the functions we have discussed so far:

- You have put in place the very best staff.
- You are working with an organizational structure that plays to individual and group strengths.
- You have started the project with sensible assignments based on a sound organizational structure.
- You have monitored progress and reallocated staff efforts to keep progress aligned across project functions.

Even having done all this, you may still need to make midcourse corrections that affect some or all of these matters. Indeed, such midcourse corrections are based in the main on the productivity or usefulness of original starting points outlined in the proposal. Where our initial hunches for organizing and launching the project are bearing fruit, we need not—and probably should not—make changes. Where we have run into challenges or problems that can only be surmounted with a different approach, we need to do so in a timely and effective fashion.

To return to the case of the archive one more time, let us say we found college-level teachers are more interested in multiple method approaches to teaching history. They may be fearful of placing all their educational bets on an archive-based teaching approach. If we discovered this during the course of the project, we might move toward a series of pairings of archive approaches with other approaches—such as lectures, small group discussions, or classical library research. Not to do so would render our study impractical, if not unusable. Importantly, we should not make this type of midcourse correction without fully communicating it to major project stakeholders. This leads to the very next point.

MAINTAIN LIAISON WITH STAKEHOLDERS AND FUNDER(S)

In part, funders gather and garner expertise in their program areas by learning what is possible and what is not from the very projects they support. We should cooperate fully in developing the educative value of our project for the sponsoring agency.

From the start, we should voluntarily check in with our program officer (PO) on how things are going. From a vantage that cuts across projects, our PO can offer useful suggestions on organization, allocation of effort, experience of other projects, and so forth. By maintaining a healthy and meaningful dialogue with the funder from the outset, a major decision—for example, making a substantial midcourse change—can be conveyed with ease and discussed with comfort. In response, you may hear how other PIs dealt with similar circumstances. You may also pick up suggestions for alternative course corrections, their optimal timing, and their import for various dimensions of the project effort.

Stated differently, where a trusting exchange relationship has developed between the PI and the funder, the PI and the project stand to benefit from a thoughtful and experienced resource on project management in general and major project decisions in particular.

SAFEGUARD THE RIGOR AND PURPOSES OF THE PROJECT

Managing a funded project is an upbeat process in which we benefit as colleagues and investigators from the experience and goodwill of those who share our enthusiasm for project-based research. We include under this rubric safeguarding the rigor and purposes of the project.

As we make choices on staff, monitor project progress, and make midcourse corrections, we need to look beyond the project to the standards by which our collective enterprise will be assessed or judged. In the end, no matter the pressing day-to-day or organizational need to which we responded with the most compelling alternative we could devise, still we must assess that alternative and its implications against the standards of research. In a way, we have made our way back to one of our three orienting principles, namely, that proper project management is critical to maintaining the rigor of the project's method's of inquiry; indeed, the former is in service to the latter.

To give credence to this view, we must hold up even our most considered project judgment(s) against the backdrop of research or other professional standards and ask if change or compromise has affected quality to an unacceptable degree. While this is a judgment call, it is the act of making the call that we are primarily concerned with at this point. Simply put, if a judgment born of standards is intentionally involved for all major project decisions and midcourse corrections, we have in place the basis for developing best project practices.

ACT AS THE PUBLIC FACE OF THE INITIATIVE

With this item and for the following three, we turn outward from the project to its more formal relationships with the public and sponsoring institution.

We associate the work of a project with an individual or two. These individuals—let us call them the PI and co-PI—are credited with developing the idea of the project, crafting the proposal, and managing the effort from inception to conclusion. No matter the degree or level of teamwork that made the project work, it is to these individuals that we turn as the public face of the initiative.

We look to them—and most consistently to the project PI—for authoritative statements of what the project has found. We may ask the PI to interpret more broadly the state of the field in which she is working or society's interest in the project and its progress. In addition to content expertise, creativity, insight, and effort, the PI as CEO is expected to present work in progress and work completed in an accessible way both to colleagues and to the broader public. To a long list of professional strengths—from conceptualizer, analyst, and writer to teacher and colleague—the project CEO must now add another: effective communicator.

In a domain of scarce resources, many professionals involved with project funding have come to believe that accurate and timely information from the project CEO must be available at all times. We reemphasize another version of this point in the final entry in this list: strategies for disseminating findings to a variety of audiences.

WRITE AND SUBMIT PROGRESS REPORTS

Progress reports are updated proposal statements. They tell the organized story of a project under way—specifically, what it proposed to do and what it actually did. Progress reports also give tentative findings, costs incurred to date, and probable time to completion. These reports are useful to the PI, the project team, and both the funder and the sponsoring college or university.

The importance of progress reports cannot be emphasized enough. In fact, they constitute an essential element of quality communication among all three parties.

- For the PI, the reports are an opportunity to take stock and modulate conceptual, organizational, and task efforts.
- For the project team, the reports are opportunities to examine together progress to date, tasks remaining, and future related visions.
- For the funder, the reports are an indication of the viability of the project and an opportunity to provide guidance and support to help achieve agreed-on outcomes.
- For the university hosting the project, the reports afford valuable insights into the workings of the project and institution-based resources (both real and perceived) that aid the timely and successful completion of the initiative.

In sum, thoughtfully written reports provide a valuable overview of progress, as well as a leg up on the completion of the final report and the publications to follow.

BE ACCOUNTABLE FOR ALL PROJECT EXPENDITURES AND COMMITMENTS

CEOs in the for-profit and not-for-profit worlds have in common the responsibility for knowing, understanding, and affirming the rationale for all expenditures and commitments their organizations make. There is no doubt in our minds that a good accountant or internal auditor will help make this responsibility easier to manage.

The idea is to link overall fiscal and managerial responsibility to timely reports and the planning and support of future project effort. In this way, the PI has a tractable means for understanding those ultimate limits on time and effort in the form of funding committed and funding remaining. These figures provide guidelines—and not judgments per se—for determining the level and scale of possible organizational choices going forward. As such, they are readily coupled to real-world project decision making that employs a common dollar metric.

DEVELOP STRATEGIES FOR DISSEMINATING FINDINGS TO A VARIETY OF AUDIENCES

Professional publications are a start. Wider public distribution to a variety of interested people is a highly desirable end that follows directly from the nature of project funding. Realizing high-purpose outcomes often depends on it. Public (i.e., governmental) and quasi-public (i.e., corporate and foundation) funds are required by law and regulation to benefit the common good. Critical to the spirit of the law is the active and effective dissemination of findings to ensure they are both available and accessible to as many people as possible. To the ultimate project authority—the PI—we turn for the intelligence, commitment, and leadership to disseminate findings to the broadest possible audience in the most timely fashion possible.

Marketing and communication expertise may well have been incorporated into the project proposal. It may also be available to the PI through university press offices or colleagues with business and/or communications backgrounds. These are people who can help the PI and the project team develop strategies for sharing project progress and outcomes with interested communities inside and outside of academe.

SERVE AS A RESOURCE FOR OTHERS

You gain in professional standing when you take all the time necessary to propose research, conduct a project, and report on findings. As others read your work, you will find that they view you as a multidimensional resource. For one, you have standing as a subject expert, someone others will want to consult on concepts and their elaboration. For another, you are seen as someone who knows how to develop an idea and garner support. Others believe that your experience can help them be successful. Finally, you are someone who knows how to follow through on an idea and bring it to completion. You will be recognized as having learned what it means to develop and manage a project, as someone who possesses considerable skills in all of the CEO responsibility areas we discussed above. To the extent that you make yourself available to others, your research experience will be of great value to them and a source of deep satisfaction for you. Serving as a resource to others is a part of the ethos of research. Though it places added demands on your time, it pays handsome professional dividends, including deservedly increased standing in a field.

Successfully Concluding a Project: Managing Multiple Directions

All told, the position of project CEO is filled with promise and excitement. The range of responsibility is wide but need not be overwhelming. Knowing that range in advance goes far in helping the PI to prepare for and embrace a role that is central to the modern research enterprise.

As we noted at the start of this chapter, *the project you led forward will produce promising leads in more directions than you originally proposed.* For example, if you began with an archive and its promising pedagogical uses, you may find yourself interested in mining the pedagogical depths of ephemera or collections of items such as posters and photographs that have social and intellectual value but lack the normal organizing attention afforded books and scholarly journals. In addition to spreading interest to cognate areas, you may also find yourself wanting to further revise and refine documents, taking extra time to collect and analyze additional data or following just one more thought to a stable intellectual conclusion.

With so many real possibilities for overrunning deadlines, as CEO you need to check your updated proposal, consider work done and work remaining, and intentionally bring your project to a sensible conclusion. This is not a pro forma exercise. It is something you need to master on the job. As the German proverb goes, *Übung macht den Meister*, or *Practice makes the master*. Perfection is not the pursuit, mastery is.

Let us put the case another way. Some projects have a way of running beyond their useful lifetimes. Others seem to stop short of producing useful outcomes. Managing a project's conclusion against a preset deadline with delimited resources and agreed-on accountability for usable outcomes is a process one can learn and successfully master on the job. To increase your learning, note the following points of reflection:

- A funded project is an intentional mix of promising ideas and a variety of external resources provided to pursue them.
- As academics, we are fully familiar with our drive to pursue ideas toward promising ends. As academic careerists, we are much less adept as a rule at knowing how to manage scarce time, people, and other resources to produce timely conclusions against preset deadlines.
- From the start of the project, we must make an effort to consciously channel what we know and rely on—curiosity, knowledge, exchange—into organized efforts that reach useful conclusions in an agreed-on period of time. We cannot and should not give up our commitment to creative scholarship.

What we must do is find the saddle point between high standards and the realistic stopping-off point, which is the conclusion of a project. While our intellectual work will go on past the conclusion of the funded initiative, the finality of that initiative must be respected from the start and acted on meticulously in the closing months of the project. While we are experts on the idea side of things and on content, methodologies, and research design, we must become expert in stewarding projects to a close. This notion embodies fiscal responsibility, regulatory and compliance responsibility (where appropriate), and strict adherence to the "90-day rule" in closing out the books, both financial and scientific. Let us consider each discipline in turn.

Fiscal responsibility requires that we check regularly on the "downflow" of resources to help ensure a safe and soft landing at the conclusion of a funded project. As a norm, we should be checking expenditures no less than every month or so from the start of the project. Starting in the final fourth month of the project, we may want to check on expenditures every 2 weeks and then in the final 2 months, every week. The information we garner from this exercise allows us to gauge the affordable collective effort remaining and how best to direct or expend it. Balancing ongoing curiosity with downflowing resources is an art we can learn and learn well.

Regulations define compliance requirements. In the end, we must be in compliance with all of the following that apply to our project:

- Patent and invention agreements
- Copyrights
- Conflict of interest guidelines
- Confidentiality requirements
- Environmental health and safety guidelines
- Biosafety requirements and, where applicable, responsible disposal requirements
- Precautions required for dealing with possible adverse events

These matters, along with the responsible conduct of research (or RCR) guidelines, are part of the funded research effort. From the first team meeting on, all members of the research group should be aware of them. As the project comes to a close, they are matters on which the PI/PD must report. The hope is that without exception, the project has raised all the compliance issues that apply and has produced written statements of compliance for inclusion in the final project report.

An Aside   Responsible Conduct of Research

Before we explain what is meant by the responsible conduct of research (RCR), let us explain that the concept is not as usefully defined as it might be. A far better orientation in our mind is toward the responsible conduct of scholarship (RCS), which connotes that research has a definite and honored place as one of many modes of scholarship and that the ethical rules that govern the conduct of scholarship must of course govern the conduct of research along with all other aspects of scholarly activity.

RCS can usefully represent our commitments as a community of scholars to the highest standards of pedagogy and teaching, creative activity, and research, where the last can take many forms—from the synthesis of bodies of classical literature to comprehensive quantitative studies to the collection and analysis of empirically based qualitative interview data. The ground rules in all cases of scholarship are essentially the same. They are the standards of honesty and care with information, respect for animate subjects, the hewing to standards of analysis and interpretation that allow others to replicate our studies through a rereading of literatures or the reanalysis of data or the rerunning of experiments and construction of new data sets.

Facilitating the contribution of research to scholarship and binding the conduct of research to guidelines that have served all forms of scholarship for millennia produces a more positive, elevating, and compelling approach to the intelligent conduct of research scholarship.

The 90-day rule refers to the closing out of accounting, scholarship, compliance, and related objectives. As the term implies, during the final 3 months of the project we need to review all of these arenas as we prepare a plan for expending final funds, addressing outstanding intellectual issues, and bringing our project into full compliance with regulatory requirements.

At the same time, we need to look at the books, articles, and other dissemination media we are working on and prepare to bring them to useful conclusions, or end points. By not waiting to the very last minute, we can organize resources to maximize project benefit to our several public audiences.

Halfway through the funding period, we should take a first stab at determining whether we will seek to conclude, extend, or augment our funded project.

No matter what our decision, we must continue to act as though the funded project under way will come to a conclusion on the scheduled date. For one thing, reports will be due at that time. For another, the project team is up and running, and we want to continue to make the very best use of the high performance level of the project organization we have built and managed.

If we receive continuation or complementary funding before the close of the project is at hand, we may wish, under some circumstances, to request a time extension. Otherwise, we counsel that the project should do its very best to conclude on time. Time does count, especially when it is related to funded inquiry designed to produce social benefit.

Chapter Summary

We want to end this chapter on the educational note we struck earlier. From the start afforded by dissertation research through research linked to postdoctoral study, the shared education of students and faculty should be the development of a professional researcher fully trained in idea development, seeking funding, and the management of research projects. As part of the professional development model, we find it is valuable, if not imperative for doctoral candidates to view their research proposals as precursors to proposing and managing funded projects. In a checklist summarizing the project management points covered in this chapter, we ask graduate and postdoctoral students and research faculty to reflect with us on the management similarities and differences between managing dissertation research and managing faculty-led funded projects.

STAFFING

Unless you have funding, you are it. You are the staff. You must manage yourself thoughtfully and resourcefully over an extended period of research and writing.

CREATING ORGANIZATION

You must a find a way to organize the project so that data, literature reviews, drafts, and rewrites come together in synthetic and holistic fashion.

DIVISION OF EFFORT

While this aspect of funded project management appears not to apply to graduate work, you will in fact be learning through your dissertation what types of effort you really enjoy and which you would really like to assign to others. The former will help you home in on the contribution you can best make to future professional project work.

MONITORING PROGRESS

This is a very useful skill, one that enables you to do work, maintain focus, and still keep an eye out for what may need addition attention or require reallocation of effort.

MIDCOURSE CORRECTION

As mentioned before, there are no altogether straight lines in research project work. This lesson, if learned in the dissertation proposal, will stand you in good stead in all your professional years. You must learn—indeed, you will learn—when and how to make directional changes in the course of an active project. In part, this is a matter of doing and then reflecting on what you have done as over and against a model, or an approach, that presumes that most everything can be planned for in advance.

MAINTAIN LIAISON WITH FUNDERS

In your dissertation project, the lesson is to maintain liaison with your adviser and committee members. There is an art to doing work, reporting on it, and incorporating feedback in a thoughtful and responsible manner. Student and professional work depend on a matrix of support that in turn depends on sharing new learning and revision in a spirit of respect and joint venture.

SAFEGUARD RIGOR AND PURPOSE

Time is always a pressure; all resources are always scarce. Maintaining the rigor and purpose of the project means not seeking shortcuts and not cutting professionally required corners. This is a tough lesson, one best learned and embedded during graduate student days.

PUBLIC FACE OF THE PROJECT

People will be interested in your work. How to describe a work in progress is demanding. Some refer to an "elevator speech," or a description of 30 seconds or less that captures the essence of what you are about. We would take you back to your idea sketch and suggest you update it every few months or so. An oral idea sketch is what people are looking for even after you have left behind a sketched-in idea in favor of a fuller, more replete idea proposal section.

PROGRESS REPORTS

You will need to provide them to you adviser and committee members. Importantly, you will need to provide them to yourself. Maintaining momentum and morale means taking time to look both backward and forward to see what you have accomplished and what remains to be done. How to capture where you are and how things are progressing in a complex project is a skill best honed in use. We would urge you to revisit the part of your proposal most affected by time—activities, timeline, budget—and capture under each where things stand. A nice touch is to include what you are learning alongside any growing sense of excitement you can honestly report about what you are learning or discovering.

ACCOUNTABILITY

While you may or may not be responsible for stewarding extramural funding, you will be answerable to yourself, your adviser, and committee for how you spent your time and effort. We suggest you embrace accountability as a helpmate. How you are spending your time, what is taking longer, where you are encountering challenges—these are matters that, once addressed, will help keep progress moving forward. Honesty in all things research includes honest accounts of how you have managed very human resources.

DISSEMINATION

Especially for the dissertation, it will be wise to consider ways to disseminate findings and results in meetings, journals, and manuscripts. You have taken your work seriously. There is a need for interested others (sometimes referred to as "interested publics" in the political science literature) to be aware of what you posed at the outset and what you learned in the end. Seeing this as a public responsibility takes it out of the realm of the ego and into the realm of responsible professional colleagueship. Given the nature of your project and its contributions to knowledge or practice, you will find ample outlets for sharing the information you have produced.

BECOME A RESOURCE

You will achieve full professional standing when you come to care about a field of inquiry, including those who currently work in it and those who may follow your lead and join up. Being a resource to others is where the pursuit of research and the art of teaching conjoin. Allow the enthusiasm for your work full display as you help others think through ideas and approaches that may well differ from your own.

6

Looking Backward and Forward

In this final chapter, we want to look both backward and forward. We want to look backward and review the major assumptions we incurred in writing this book. Articulating these assumptions will help highlight the strengths and the limitations of what we have written. This we will do briefly. Looking forward is what we want to emphasize.

We want to look broadly at the future of funded research in two interconnected ways. We wish to emphasize the key roles of international research opportunities, and we want to address the increasingly major role research infrastructure is destined to play. The ever-widening international context of research calls out compliance and research support structures as never before. Our research teams of graduate, postdoctoral, and faculty researchers will do well to acquaint themselves with the future face of funded research worldwide.

The Major Assumptions We Incurred

Of all the assumptions we incurred, among the most major are four. One is the cast we placed on the relationship between applicant and funder. We acted as though the funder always understands and acts on the intentions of the applicant, and is always attentive to what the applicant brings to the table. We also acted as though the applicant is always straightforward and up-front about interests, capabilities, and institutional support. While these assumptions are not always met, they are assumptions that we believe should drive the relationship between applicant and funder toward an ever more ethically positive engagement.

The second major assumption we incurred revolved around the idea development process. We assumed—let us say, we asserted—that the process of moving an idea forward almost always involved multiple individuals in a mutually supportive relationship. Quite clearly, there are individuals who can carry on their work in isolation from colleagues and still produce quality work; however, we have come to believe that even individually driven projects in science, humanities, or social science benefit from multiple perspectives represented by multiple colleagues. Our assumption that proposals and projects benefit from group process is an assumption that we believe in and act on, but it is an assumption, nevertheless.

The third major assumption is that seeking and gaining research funding is a rational process that begins with ideas, continues with database searches, and comes to culmination in a live relationship between applicant and funder. We assume and believe this cycle of events helps to increase the probability of better ideas being placed before appropriate funders in a form that increases receptivity to and understanding of them. Of course, there are times when individuals meet funders, drop a line about an interest, and both are off and running toward a project grant. That is the exception that makes the point all the stronger that time taken with ideas, database searches, letters of inquiry, and the like improve both the proposed work and the chances of successful funding.

A fourth major assumption is that there is a discontinuity between training for academic work and training for the conduct of funded research. No matter how well one does in the former regimen, there is no guarantee that the rigor of analysis and the depth and breadth of subject competence will translate into the management skills required to carry out a funded project in an orderly and successful way. This, for us, is a thoroughgoing assumption; one that guided us at every turn in developing and writing this book.

International Research and Its Support Structures

Over the past several years, one of the authors (Carfora), in his capacity as a recognized expert on international research administration and management, has received many inquiries from colleagues in the United States and abroad seeking advice on a range of matters, including but not limited to the following:

1. Recommendations for strategies and best practices for bringing together faculty, postdoctoral scholars, graduate students, senior university officers, and research administrators and managers around the preparation of high-profile international research collaborations that could then be submitted as interinstitutional proposals to multinational governmental agencies, foundations, corporations, professional and scholarly associations, and other potential sponsors.

2. Recommendations of top-notch translational services, as well as guidance on cross-cultural questions about a particular country's professional ethos and bureaucratic and operational traditions.

3. Guidance on a host of compliance issues, including the following:
   - Contractual and policy-related guidance on full economic costing
   - Allowable costs and documentation of in-country transactions
   - Payment terms and required flowdowns—that is contractual terms and conditions that flow down from funder to recipient to subrecipient, where applicable
   - Appropriate certifications and assurances
   - Publication rights
   - Intellectual property
   - Technology transfer
   - Material transfer agreements
   - Human subject protection and animal care/use
   - Confidentiality agreements
   - Ownership and disposition of equipment
   - General accounting and auditing issues
   - Use of independent contractors
   - Subrecipient monitoring of those who receive subcontracts from the primary recipient of funding
   - Taxation
   - Insurance
   - Governing law, dispute resolution, and use of arbitration
   - Personal safety and security concerns
   - Export controls

This rather broad list—though far from exhaustive—provides an example of the topical and thematic concerns behind the growing interest in international research administration. In addition to all of the above, non-Americans often ask for specific guidance involving language and clauses in proposed agreements, particularly seeking clarification on indemnification, intellectual property, and publication rights (again to name but a few). They are also anxious to learn more about research administration in the United States—especially with an eye toward those offices providing both pre- and post-award services—so they can better understand the operational nuances of American research administration.

Queries from American and international colleagues—particularly from senior research managers—often seek guidance on how to best provide training and education to university-based faculty and staff, as well as how to ensure best practices and maintain institutional knowledge critical to international research administration. Four avenues are available to researchers and administrators wanting to maximize training, education, and professional development opportunities (Carfora & Wallen, 2008).

First, many learning opportunities are available through international associations, such as (in alphabetical order) the Association of Commonwealth Universities (ACU), Association of Research Managers and Administrators (ARMA), Australasian Research Management Society (ARMS), Canadian

Association of University Research Administrators (CAURA), Danish Association for Research Managers and Administrators (DARMA), European Association of Research Managers and Administrators (EARMA), International Network of Research Management Societies (INORMS), National Council of University Research Administrators (NCURA), Southern African Research and Innovation Management Association (SARIMA), Swiss Association of Research Managers and Administrators (SARMA), Society of Research Administrators (SRA), and West African Research and Innovative Management Association (WARIMA). All offer training, education and professional development opportunities either online, at annual meetings, or via specialized conferences or workshops. Second, many online materials are available from governmental agencies and associations that serve the international research administration community. One of the best places to access these online resources is through NCURA's International Neighborhood.

Third, as international research cooperation and collaboration spreads, sponsored research offices will need to maintain a range of up-to-date resources, including books, articles, white papers, documents, reports, policies, and pertinent government and nongovernmental items (in print and online). Such collections will make available a large body of knowledge that will help facilitate institutional knowledge and support staff training and development necessary for the conduct of international research initiatives. Fourth, the cultivation of an international network of research administrators who can provide perspective and experientially based insight on a variety of transnational themes is invaluable. It is essential for sponsored project offices to help staff members develop their proficiency in the business side of international research administration and thus develop their confidence in the cross-cultural nuances that underwrite successful international collaborations.

Taking a broad look into the future, as globally integrated research administration becomes a growing feature of our professional future, we will see the establishment of offices for international collaborations. They will no doubt appear first at larger research universities where further development of guidelines and best practices for managing international projects will take place. As has been the tradition in our profession, such endeavors will help elevate the standards by which we manage international projects at all our respective organizations. Finally, we will also see greater collaboration among colleges and universities, governmental agencies, and professional and academic associations in the United States and abroad (particularly in Africa, Asia, and South America) as research administrators and managers around the globe look for applied solutions and professional development opportunities that transcend national boundaries.

Conclusion

If we may be so bold, the idea of the university was from its start, some 9 or 10 centuries ago, a place that nurtures ideas. In our time, the university has become a place that nurtures ideas, not only in courses and conferences but also in projects, programs, and products that enjoy extra-university support. This widening of idea development and its relationship to societal and scientific priorities is relatively recent in the history of higher education.

For the part that all of us get to play in the unfolding and development of this very welcome trend, we offer our collective thanks. Never before in the history of higher education and therefore in the history of civilization, have so many spent such concerted time, effort, and resources on addressing social and scientific concerns. We trust that this book will help make that experience more understandable, enjoyable, and effective.

Recommended Resources and Selected Bibliography

I n response to requests for user-friendly books and guides to grant writing, proposal development, grant and contract administration, fund-raising, and philanthropy in general, below are a range of comprehensive resources— both new and old—we have found extremely useful over the years. Each strives in its own way to make one's entry into grant writing, fund-raising, and the exciting domain of research and sponsored programs administration easier and more productive. We trust you also will discover valuable sources in this list for both the seasoned "grantgetter" and the novice "grantseeker."

Alley, M. (1996). *The craft of scientific writing* (3rd ed.). New York: Springer.

Anderson, A. (1996). *Ethics for fundraisers*. Bloomington: Indiana University Press.

Barbato, J., & Furlich, D. (2000). *Writing for a good cause: The complete guide to crafting proposals and other persuasive pieces for nonprofits*. Hoboken, NJ: Wiley.

Bauer, D. G. (1989). *Administering grants, contracts, and funds: Evaluating and improving your grants system*. New York: Macmillan.

Bauer, D. G. (1994). *Successful grants program management*. New York: Scholastic.

Bauer, D. G. (1995). *The complete grants sourcebook for higher education*. Phoenix, AZ: American Council on Education/Oryx Press.

Bauer, D. G. (2001). *How to evaluate and improve your grants effort* (2nd ed.). Phoenix, AZ: American Council on Education/Oryx Press.

Bauer, D. G. (2003). *The "how to" grants manual: Successful grantseeking techniques for obtaining public and private grants* (5th ed.). Westport, CT: Praeger.

Belcher, J. C., & Jacobsen, J. M. (1992). *From idea to funded project: Grant proposals that work* (4th ed.). Phoenix, AZ: Oryx Press.

Bloomberg, L.D., & Volpe, M. (2008). *Completing your qualitative dissertation: A roadmap from beginning to end*. Thousand Oaks, CA: Sage.

Blum, L. (1996). *Complete guide to getting a grant: How to turn your ideas into dollars*. New York: Wiley.

Bowman, J. P., & Branchaw, B. P. (1992). *How to write proposals that produce*. Phoenix, AZ: Oryx Press.

Brewer, E., Achilles, C. M., & Fuhriman, J. R. (1995). *Finding funding: Grantwriting and project management from start to finish.* Thousand Oaks, CA: Corwin.

Brown, L. G., & Brown, M. J. (2001). *Demystifying grant seeking: What you REALLY need to do to get grants* (2nd ed.). San Francisco: Jossey-Bass.

Browning, B. A. (2001). *Grant writing for dummies.* Indianapolis, IN: Wiley.

Carfora, J., & Wallen, D. (2008). Building toward successful international research collaborations. *Sponsored research administration: A guide to effective strategies and recommended practices.* Washington, DC: National Council of University Research Administrators and Atlantic Information Services.

Carlson, M. (1995). *Winning grants step-by-step: Support centers of America's complete workbook for planning, developing, and writing successful proposals.* San Francisco: Jossey-Bass.

Carlson, M., & Clarke, C. (2000). *Team-based fundraising step-by-step: A practical guide to improving results through teamwork.* San Francisco: Jossey-Bass.

Ciconte, B. L., & Jacob, J. (2001). *Fundraising basics: A complete guide* (2nd ed.). Boston: Jones and Bartlett.

Coley, S. M., & Xcheinberg, A. (2000). *Proposal writing* (2nd ed.). Thousand Oaks, CA: Sage.

Corporation for Public Broadcasting. *Grant proposal writing tips.* Retrieved November 2, 2009, from http://www.cpb.org/grants/grantwriting.html

Davis, M. (2004). *Scientific papers and presentations* (2nd ed.). San Diego, CA: Academic Press.

Day, R. A., & Gastel, B. (2006). *How to write and publish a scientific paper* (6th ed.). Westport, CT: Greenwood Press.

Dermer, J. (1975). *How to write successful foundation presentations.* New York: Public Service Materials Center.

Duronio, M. A. (1991). *Effective fund raising in higher education: Ten success stories.* San Francisco: Jossey-Bass.

Foundation Center. *Proposal writing short course (Part one).* Retrieved November 2, 2009, from http://foundationcenter.org/getstarted/tutorials/shortcourse/index.html

Friedland, A. J., & Folt, C. L. (2000). *Writing successful science proposals.* New Haven, CT: Yale University Press.

Garfunkel, H. (1991). *Studies in ethnomethodology.* Englewood Cliffs, NJ: Prentice-Hall.

Geever, J. C. (2004). *The foundation center's guide to proposal writing* (4th ed.). New York: Foundation Center.

Gerin, W. (2006). *Writing the NIH grant proposal: A step-by-step guide.* Thousand Oaks, CA: Sage.

Gilpatrick, E. (1989). *Grants for nonprofit organizations: A guide to funding and grant writing.* Westport, CT: Praeger.

Gitlin, L. N., & Lyons, K. J. (2008). *Successful grant writing strategies for health and human service professionals* (3rd ed.). New York: Springer.

Gronbjerg, K. A. (1993). *Understanding nonprofit funding: Managing revenues in social services and community development organizations.* San Francisco: Jossey-Bass.

Hailman, J. P., & Strier, K. B. (2006). *Planning, proposing and presenting science effectively: A guide for graduate students and researchers in the behavioral sciences and biology* (2nd ed.). Cambridge, UK: Cambridge University Press.

Hall, M. R. (1993). *The dean's role in fund raising.* Baltimore: Johns Hopkins University Press.

Hall, M. S., & Howlett, S. (2003). *Getting funded: The complete guide to writing grant proposals* (4th ed.). Portland, OR: Portland State University, Extended Studies, Continuing Education Press.

Hamper, R. J., & Baugh, L. S. (1996). *Handbook for writing proposals.* Lincolnwood, IL: NTC Business Books.

Harris, T. (1999). *International fund raising for not-for-profits: A country-by-country profile.* New York: Wiley.

Henson, K. T. (2003). Debunking some myths about grant writing. *Chronicle of Higher Education.* Retrieved November 2, 2009, from http://chronicle.com/article/Debunking-Some-Myths-About-/45256/

Henson, K. T. (2004). *Grant writing in higher education.* Boston: Allyn & Bacon.

Krit, R. L. (1991). *The fund-raising handbook.* Glenview, IL: Scott Foresman.

Kulakowski, E. C., & Chronister, L. U. (Eds.). (2006). *Research administration and management.* Sudbury, MA: Jones and Bartlett.

Lauffer, A. (1997). *Grants, etc.* (2nd ed.). Thousand Oaks, CA: Sage.

Lefferts, R. (1990). *Getting a grant in the 1990s: How to write successful grant proposals.* New York: Prentice Hall.

Levine, S. J. (2005). *Guide for writing a funding proposal.* Retrieved April 15, 2008, from http://www.learnerassociates.net/proposal/

Lewis, H. G. (1989). *How to write powerful fund-raising letters.* Chicago: Pluribus Press.

Locke, L. R., Spirduso, W. W., & Silverman, S. J. (2007). *Proposals that work: A guide for planning dissertations and grant proposals* (5th ed.). Thousand Oaks, CA: Sage.

Matthews, J. R., & Mathews, R. W. (2007). *Successful scientific writing: A step-by-step guide for the biological and medical sciences.* Cambridge, UK: Cambridge University Press.

Miner, J. T., & Miner, L. E. (2005). *Models of proposal planning and writing.* Westport, CT: Praeger.

Miner, L. E., & Miner, J. T. (2003). *Proposal planning and writing* (3rd ed.). Westport, CT: Greenwood Press.

Murray, K., & Mutz, J. (2005). *Fundraising for dummies* (2nd ed.). Hoboken, NJ: Wiley.

National Institute of Allergy and Infectious Diseases. (2008). *All about grants tutorials.* Retrieved April 15, 2009, from http://www.niaid.nih.gov/ncn/grants/default.htm

National Institutes of Health, Office of Extramural Research. (2007). *Grant writing tips sheet.* Retrieved November 2, 2009, from http://grants.nih.gov/grants/grant_ tips.htm

National Science Foundation. (n.d.). *A guide for proposal writing.* Retrieved April 2, 2008, from http://www.nsf.gov/pubs/2004/nsf04016/nsf04016.pdf

National Science Foundation. (2007). *Grant proposal guide.* Retrieved November 2, 2009, from http://www.nsf.gov/publications/pub_summ.jsp?ods_key=gpg

New, C. C., & Quick, J. A. (2003). *How to write a grant proposal.* Hoboken, NJ: Wiley.

Odendahl, T., & O'Neill, M. (1994). *Women and power in the nonprofit sector.* San Francisco: Jossey-Bass.

Ogden, T. E., & Goldberg, I. A. (2002). *Research proposals: A guide to success* (3rd ed.). San Diego, CA: Academic Press.

Orlich, D. C. (1996). *Designing successful grant proposals.* Alexandria, VA: Association for Supervision and Curriculum Development.

Porter, R. (2007). Why academics have a hard time writing good grant proposals. *Journal of Research Administration, 38,* 161–167.

Powell, W. W. (1987). *The nonprofit sector: A research handbook.* New Haven, CT: Yale University Press.

Prince, R. A., & File, K. M. (1994). *The seven faces of philanthropy: A new approach to cultivating donors.* San Francisco: Jossey-Bass.

Przeworski, A., & Salomon, F. (1995). *The art of writing proposals: Some candid suggestions for applicants to the social science research council competitions.* Retrieved November 2, 2009, from http://www.ssrc.org/ workspace/images/crm/new_publication_3/{7a9cb4f4-815f-de11-bd80-001cc477ec70}.pdf

Quick, J. A., & New, C. C. (2000). *Grant winner's toolkit: Project management and evaluation.* New York: Wiley.

Quick, J. A., & New, C. C. (2001). *Grant seekers budget toolkit: Project management and evaluation.* New York: Wiley.

Reif-Lehrer, D. (1989). *Going for the gold: Some do's and dont's for grant seekers.* Rockville, MD: National Institute on Alcohol Abuse and Alcoholism, U.S. Dept. of Health and Human Services, Public Health Service, Alcohol, Drug Abuse, and Mental Health Administration.

Reif-Lehrer, D. (1989). *Writing a successful grant application* (2nd ed.). Boston: Jones and Bartlett.

Reif-Lehrer, D. (2005). *Grant application writer's handbook* (4th ed.). Boston: Jones and Bartlett.

Richey, J. B. (1994). Budgeting for international projects in-country: Operations and long-term residential Assignments. *Journal of the Society of Research Administrators, 25*(3), 13–37.

Richey, J. B. (1993). Crafting contracts for international projects. *Journal of the Society of Research Administrators, 25*(3), 5–23.

Ries, J. B., & Leukefeld, C. G. (1998). *Research funding guidebook: Getting it, managing it, renewing it.* Thousand Oaks, CA: Sage.

Rosso, H. A. (1996). *Rosso on fund raising: Lessons from a master's lifetime experience.* San Francisco: Jossey-Bass.

Ruskin, K. B., & Achilles, C. M. (1995). *Grantwriting, fundraising, and partnerships: Strategies that work.* Thousand Oaks, CA: Corwin.

Schumacher, D. (1992). *Get funded! A practical guide for scholars seeking research support from business.* Newbury Park, CA: Sage.

Seymour, H. J. (1966). *Designs for fund-raising principles, patterns, techniques.* New York: McGraw-Hill.

Snyder, A. (2007). Ten ways to write a better grant: Sure you need a good idea, but it's more than that. *The Scientist, 21*(1), 71.

Strunk, W., Jr., & White, E. B. (2005). *The elements of style.* New York: Penguin Press.

Tenbrunsel, T. W. (1982). *The fund raising resource manual.* New York: Prentice Hall.

Thackrey, D. (n.d.). *University of Michigan proposal writer's guide.* Retrieved November 2, 2009, from http://www.drda.umich.edu/proposals/pwg/pwgintro.html

Weinstein, S. (1999). *Complete guide to fund-raising management.* New York: Wiley.

Wells, M. (2005). *Grantwriting beyond the basics, book 1: Proven strategies professionals use to make their proposals work.* Portland, OR: Portland State University Extended Studies, Continuing Education Press.

White, V. P. (1983). *Grant proposals that succeeded.* New York: Plenum Press.

Worth, M. J. (2002). *New strategies for educational fund raising.* Westport, CT: Praeger.

Yang, O. O. (2005). *Guide to effective grant writing: How to write an effective NIH application.* New York: Springer Science and Business Media.

Proposal Writing Resources Available Via the Web

All About Grants Tutorials (NIAID), http://www.niaid.nih.gov/ncn/grants/default
.htm

The Art of Writing Proposals: Some Candid Suggestions for Applicants to Social
Science Research Council Competitions, by A. Przeworksi and F. Salomon
(Social Science Research Council), http://fellowships.ssrc.org/art_of_writing_
proposals/

Basic Elements of Grant Writing (Corporation for Public Broadcasting), http://www
.cpb.org/grants/grantwriting.html

Debunking Some Myths About Grant Writing, by Kenneth T. Henson (*Chronicle of
Higher Education*), http://chronicle.com/jobs/2003/06/2003062601c.htm

Developing and Writing Grant Proposals, The Catalog of Federal Domestic Assistance,
http://chronicle.com/article/Debunking-Some-Myths-About-/45256/

Grant Writing Tips Sheet (NIH), http://grants.nih.gov/grants/grant_tips.htm

Guide for Writing a Funding Proposal, by S. J. Levine (Michigan State University),
http://www.learnerassociates.net/proposal/

New Investigator Guide to NIH Funding (NIAID), http://www.niaid.nih.gov/ncn/
grants/new/default.htm

Proposal Writer's Guide, by D. Thackrey (University of Michigan), http://www.drda
.umich.edu/proposals/pwg/pwgintro.html

Proposal Writing Short Course (The Foundation Center), http://foundationcenter.org/
getstarted/tutorials/shortcourse/index.html

Ten Ways to Write a Better Grant: Sure You Need a Good Idea, But It's More Than
That, by Alison Snyder (*The Scientist*), http://www.thescientist.com/article/
display/38046/

STARTING OUT VIA NATIONAL INSTITUTES OF HEALTH (NIH)

Application Essentials, http://www.niaid.nih.gov/ncn/grants/new/new09.htm

Are You "New"? http://www.niaid.nih.gov/ncn/grants/new/new07.htm

The Art of Grantsmanship, http://www.hfsp.org/how/ArtOfGrants.htm

Do You Qualify for Independent Support? http://www.niaid.nih.gov/ncn/grants/
new/new06.htm

Getting to Know NIH, http://www.niaid.nih.gov/ncn/grants/new/new02.htm

GrantProposal.com, http://www.grantproposal.com/

GrantsNet, http://sciencecareers.sciencemag.org/funding

NIH's Mission—Why It Matters to You, http://www.niaid.nih.gov/ncn/grants/new/
new08.htm

Perspective on Peer Review, http://www.niaid.nih.gov/ncn/grants/new/new05.htm

Putting Grants in Context, http://www.niaid.nih.gov/ncn/grants/new/new04.htm

Starting a Research Career, http://www.niaid.nih.gov/ncn/grants/new/new03.htm

Staying Informed, http://www.niaid.nih.gov/ncn/grants/new/new12.htm

What Award Should You Apply For? http://www.niaid.nih.gov/ncn/grants/new/
new10.htm

What's an R01? http://www.niaid.nih.gov/ncn/grants/new/new11.htm

SHAPING YOUR STRATEGY VIA NIH

Choosing a Topic, http://www.niaid.nih.gov/ncn/grants/new/new14.htm
Deciding the Parameters of Your Request, http://www.niaid.nih.gov/ncn/grants/new/new16.htm
How Funding Opportunities Work, http://www.niaid.nih.gov/ncn/grants/new/new18.htm
How to Plan an Appropriate Budget, http://www.niaid.nih.gov/ncn/grants/new/new17.htm
How to Write a Grant Application, http://www.niaid.nih.gov/ncn/grants/write/write_pf.htm
Plan Ahead for Electronic Application, http://www.niaid.nih.gov/ncn/grants/new/new19.htm
Planning Your Application, http://www.niaid.nih.gov/ncn/grants/new/new13.htm
Should You Be One of Many PIs? http://www.niaid.nih.gov/ncn/grants/new/new15.htm

CREATING AND SUBMITTING YOUR APPLICATION VIA NIH

Getting Oriented, http://www.niaid.nih.gov/ncn/grants/new/new21.htm
Grant Proposal Guide (National Science Foundation), http://www.nsf.gov/pubs/2004/nsf042/nsf04_2.pdf
Grant Writing for New Applicants, http://www.niaid.nih.gov/ncn/grants/new/new22.htm
A Guide for Proposal Writing (National Science Foundation), http://www.nsf.gov/pubs/2004/nsf04016/nsf04016.pdf
Philanthropy Northwest, http://www.philanthropynw.org/s_pnw/index.asp
Programs for New PIs, http://www.niaid.nih.gov/ncn/grants/new/new25.htm
Selected Pages From All About Grants, http://www.niaid.nih.gov/ncn/grants/new/new23.htm
Submitting the Application, http://www.niaid.nih.gov/ncn/grants/new/new24.htm
Web Resources, http://www.niaid.nih.gov/ncn/grants/new/new26.htm

SELECTED NIH RESOURCES ON QUALITATIVE RESEARCH VIA NIH

Analysis and Use of Qualitative Data, http://www.nida.nih.gov/pdf/monographs/monograph166/292_309.pdf
Qualitative Methods in Drug Abuse and HIV Research, http://www.nida.nih.gov/pdf/monographs/157.pdf
Qualitative Methods in Environmental Health Research, http://www.ehponline.org/members/2003/6196/6196.pdf
Qualitative Methods in Health Research: Opportunities and Considerations in Application and Review, http://obssr.od.nih.gov/Documents/Publications/Qualitative.PDF

SELECTED NSF RESOURCES ON QUALITATIVE RESEARCH VIA NIH

Analyzing Qualitative Data, http://www.ehr.nsf.gov/EHR/REC/pubs/NSF97-153/CHAP_4.HTM

Frequently Asked Questions on Proposal Preparation and Award Administration, http://www.nsf.gov/pubs/2003/nsf03041/faqs03_041.pdf

Overview of Qualitative Methods and Analytic Techniques, http://www.ehr.nsf.gov/ EHR/REC/pubs/NSF97-153/CHAP_3.HTM

2002 User-Friendly Handbook for Project Evaluation, http://www.nsf.gov/pubs/2002/ nsf02057/nsf02057.pdf

User-Friendly Handbook for Mixed Method Evaluations, http://www.ehr.nsf.gov/EHR/ REC/pubs/NSF97-153/pdf/mm_eval.pdf

Index

ABOUT THE AUTHOR

John Spearman (Jake to his friends and colleagues) is a Latin teacher and coach at a prestigious New England boarding school. Before joining the world of academia, Spearman had been a sales and marketing executive for 25 years. In 2006, he walked away from an executive position with a Fortune 500 company to return to school. He earned his M.A. in Latin in a calendar year and began teaching thereafter.

He began writing as a hobby. His first four books, the Halberd series, have been well-received. This book is the second of a new series, unrelated to the earlier books.

Made in the USA
Columbia, SC
18 May 2022

60573302R00120